Aerobatics
Principles and
Practice

DAVID ROBSON

Airlife
England

Aerobatics – Principles and Practice

Nothing in this handbook supersedes any legislation, rules, regulations or procedures contained in any operational document issued by Her Majesty's Stationery Office, the Civil Aviation Authority, the manufacturers of aircraft, engines and systems, or by the operators of aircraft throughout the world.

Copyright © 2001 Aviation Theory Centre

ISBN 1 84037 272 9

First Edition published 1999
First Airlife Edition published 2001

Cover Photo: Garry Veroude
Graphics & Typesetting: Aviation Theory Centre, Melbourne, Australia

Printed and bound in Great Britain by Biddles Ltd., Guildford and King's Lynn

Airlife Publishing Ltd

101 Longden Road, Shrewsbury SY3 9EB, Shropshire, England

E-mail: airlife@airlifebooks.com
Website www.airlifebooks.com

Author

David Robson is a career aviator having been nurtured on balsa wood, dope (the legal kind) and tissue paper. As an Air Training Corps cadet he was awarded a flying scholarship and made his first solo flight in a Chipmunk, with the Surrey and Kent Flying Club at Biggin Hill, shortly after his seventeenth birthday. He made his first parachute jump with the British Parachute Club at Fairoaks at the age of sixteen.

His family returned to Australia in 1962. He joined the Royal Australian Air Force in 1965 and served for twenty-one years as a fighter pilot and test pilot. He flew over 1,000 hours on Mirages and 500 on Sabres. He completed a tour in Vietnam, as a Forward Air Controller, with the United States Air Force.

He was a member of the *Deltas*, a seven-aircraft formation aerobatic team, which flew his favorite aircraft, the Mirage fighter. This team was specially formed to celebrate the fiftieth anniversary of the RAAF in 1971.

He completed the Empire Test Pilot's course at Boscombe Down in 1972, flying everything from gliders, through the Chipmunk, Argosy and Canberra, to the magnificent Hunter and English Electric Lightning. Memorable moments include passing the Concorde test aircraft in flight, inverted spinning in the Hunter and in-flight refuelling the Lightning from a Victor tanker over the North Sea.

After retiring from the Air Force, David became a civilian instructor and lecturer. During 1986–8 he was the editor of the *Aviation Safety Digest* which won the Flight Safety Foundation's prestigious international award.

He spent over ten years at the Australian Aviation College at Parafield as the Director of Pilot Training and Manager, Business Development. He introduced the Mudry CAP 10B aerobatic training aircraft to Australia. He holds a First Class Airline Transport Pilot's Licence and a Grade 1 Instructor's Rating. He was awarded the Australian Aviation Safety Foundation's Certificate of Air Safety for 1998. He loves aeroplanes, aerobatics and instructing – and he still dreams of, one day, flying a Spitfire.

Acknowledgements

My thanks to:

Monsieur Auguste Mudry is one of the great men of French aviation. Indeed he has been called the Enzo Ferrari of France because of his lifetime dedication to the manufacture of the best-handling aerobatic aircraft in the world. I was fortunate to be able to meet Mr Mudry on several occasions when I was selecting aircraft for the Australian Aviation College.

Avions Mudry produced world-class competition aerobatic aircraft, and the very best aerobatic training aircraft, the CAP 10B. The CAP 10B was developed from the Piel Emeraude as a basic trainer for the French Air Force. The design has been so successful that it has remained in production for 25 years without major change. The wings of the CAP 10B are covered with plywood skins, which are spliced with the same care as a violin. The aircraft were built at a rate of one per month and Mr Mudry was able to visit the factory every day and personally inspect (and pat) each aircraft as it was built. Avions Mudry is no longer, but the aircraft continue to be built at a new facility, CAP Aviation in Darois, France.

I was privileged to know Mr Mudry, to fly his aircraft and to share his Calvados.

David Pilkington has been in the aviation industry since 1966 when he started flying and became an aeronautical engineering student at RMIT, then later at Cranfield College of Aeronautics. His flying interests are purely aerobatic – Australian Advanced Aerobatic Champion, Pitts aerobatic formation team, low-level aerobatic testing officer, and aerobatic instructor. His flying and engineering interests were combined for the development of the Laser. In 1995, he joined Aviat in the US as Vice President, Engineering, and as test/demonstration pilot for the new Pitts and the Husky.

David has since returned to Melbourne, where he worked for Boeing Australia and lately British Aerospace Australia as an engineer. He moonlights on weekends as a flight instructor, teaching aerobatics in anything from the Cessna Aerobat to the Pitts S-2A – in between wringing-out his Laser.

Dominique Roland is a former test pilot for Avions Mudry, member of the French National Aerobatic Team, Breitling world title holder and now Chief Executive of CAP Aviation which produces the CAP 10, CAP 232, and the tandem-seat, high-performance CAP 222.

Dominique was brave enough to allow me to fly his personal competition aircraft, the CAP 231EX – for which I am eternally grateful. It was a wonderful experience. It had a ratchet mechanism on the harness to really tighten you in and ski boots which locked into the rudder pedals for negative-g manoeuvring. It rolled at more than 400 degrees a second – although I did not nearly test its full capability.

Preface

Why This Book Was Written

This book is the result of two emotions:

- enthusiasm for flying, and
- concern for incomplete pilot training.

A pilot moves in a three-dimensional world and I believe it is negligent not to train a pilot to be able to place an aircraft in any attitude and to recover safely from any attitude. In order to do this, both the training curriculum and the specifications for training aeroplanes need to be addressed.

Also, aerobatic flight is sheer fun. The thrill, challenge and enjoyment of aerobatic flight is unmatched by any other sport. It is like driving a racing car – in three dimensions.

Training Curriculum

I was fortunate to learn to fly on Chipmunks when the flying training syllabus produced a complete, three-dimensional pilot. Military flying then reinforced the essential foundation of manoeuvring flight and all aspects of aircraft control.

Reading of the many occasions where the pilot *lost* control often led me to wonder about their basic flight training. A pilot should never *lose* control.

Large aircraft filled with passengers also had *upsets* where the bank angle, and sometimes the pitch attitude, exceeded 90°. Recovery from these situations can be marginal – to say the least.

I watched videos and even witnessed air display accidents that simply shouldn't have occurred. I noticed, in several training manuals, discrepancies in the description and technique for aerobatic flight that simply could not be left unanswered.

Training Aircraft

The ability to properly train a pilot also depends on the availability of a suitable training aircraft. The lack of such aircraft and the acceptance by licensing authorities of this lack has had an effect of the completeness of pilot training for the past three or four or five decades.

The accident rate on our roads is not being contained by further regulation. Nor is it with aviation accidents. The only way to lower the rate is by better training – and this requires suitable vehicles. Aircraft such as the Tiger Moth, Chipmunk and the Stearman were effective trainers because they developed good hand/eye coordination, an awareness of and a respect for airspeed, a discipline for flightpath control and a sensitivity to surface winds. They were a challenge to fly accurately and well. They taught correct habit patterns and responses – essential to the automatic correction of flightpath or airspeed deviations.

The touring aircraft that currently populate the majority of the world's training fleets are not suitable trainers for other than cross-country and procedural training.

For the preparation of this book, indeed for the past ten years, I was fortunate to have access to the CAP 10, which has all of the attributes of the classic trainer. Consequently, the descriptions in this book are biased towards the behaviour of that aircraft. Obviously, your aircraft will have individual characteristics which will require variations in the techniques or entry speeds. However, the principles remain the same.

Airmanship

Why Talk About Airmanship?

The complete pilot training *package* includes learning how to recognise and control attitude – not only that of the aircraft but also that of the pilot. The pilot's mental attitude is what we used to call *airmanship.*

Aviating is a motor skill and it is a form of motor sport. Airmanship could be called aeronautical sportsmanship – it's about following the rules of the game, striving for higher standards, staying safe and courteously sharing the sky with other *drivers.*

When I was a youngster, my father gave me a little book on *seamanship.* It held *secrets* of flag signals, tying knots, laying coils of rope to avoid snagging, rules of the road and procedures and protocols for the operations of watercraft.

More than ever we need a similar guide for airmanship, but more importantly we in the profession need to profess it and to set an example.

I hope that flying instructors will keep alive the concept of airmanship. Otherwise, we are in danger of losing the skill, status, respect, courtesy and pride in our very special profession of aviation.

Contents

Introduction

Why Learn Aerobatics?

The practice of aerobatics develops sensitivity, feel, judgement and anticipation – (as the actress said to the bishop).

A tram or train can move in two directions but in only one dimension, backwards or forwards, along its track. A motor vehicle or a boat can move in two dimensions, backwards, forwards, left and right (making their own tracks). A submarine can move in three dimensions albeit in a limited way – no inverted flight (hopefully). Only an aircraft can truly move in three-dimensional space. Yet, most pilots never learn how to fully manoeuvre the aircraft in this three-dimensional space. Certainly, we can take off, climb, turn, descend and land, but that's a very small part of the total flight envelope of which most aircraft, and most pilots, are capable.

Learning aerobatics not only allows you to explore the full envelope of the aircraft, it considerably enhances confidence in your own ability and that of the aircraft.

Student pilots, having learnt the basic manoeuvres, noticeably improve in their general handling of the aircraft. Aerobatics develop a feel and sensitivity for the aircraft and a de-sensitivity to manoeuvring flight. They develop an instinctive awareness of attitude and the quickest way back to straight-and-level, controlled flight.

Because an aircraft manoeuvres in three-dimensional space, a pilot should be capable of placing the aircraft into any attitude and recovering safely from any attitude.

There have been several instances, even with an aircraft the size of a Jumbo, where autopilot malfunctions, volcanic eruptions or upsets due to wake turbulence have put the aircraft in a situation where the bank angle has exceeded 90 degrees and the pitch attitude has reached 30 degrees or more, nose-down. A pilot who has undergone even the basics of aerobatic training is more likely to recover correctly. There have been instances where this training has led to a successful recovery. Also, the probability of recovering safely and without further damage to the aircraft is enhanced.

Last but not least, a good reason for learning aerobatics is the sheer enjoyment of it all. There is nothing more exhilarating than flying an aerobatic aircraft and putting together a smoothly coordinated, balanced and well-performed sequence of aerobatic manoeuvres.

Above all, the learning of aerobatics develops respect for the aircraft and yourself – your abilities, your capabilities and your limitations. Aerobatics is exciting flight. No pilot should miss the opportunity to at least fly the basic, positive-*g* manoeuvres.

Let's go for it.

Aerobatic 'Wisdom'

There is no situation in aerobatic flight from which you will not be able to recover – provided you don't allow yourself to get into such a position with insufficient altitude.

Don't fly with, or learn from, anyone who is not a qualified aerobatic instructor.

Don't perform aerobatics in an aircraft that is not specifically approved for aerobatics.

Don't commence an aerobatic manoeuvre unless you are certain of completing it above your approved minimum height and with sufficient remaining energy to zoom.

Don't commence manoeuvring without a prior self-briefing or without mental preparation.

Don't commence manoeuvring without briefing your passengers.

Don't commence manoeuvring without completing the HASELL checks and clearing turns or wing-overs.

Don't commence manoeuvring unless you know the required horizontal and vertical airspace is clear of other aircraft.

Don't perform ad-hoc or ad-lib sequences – nor beat-ups.

Don't manoeuvre a new type without a check pilot or at least at a safe altitude which allows for unexpected responses.

Don't spin an aircraft unless you are familiar with its correct (and perhaps, unique) entry and recovery procedures, and you are certain that it is correctly loaded.

Don't perform aerobatics, especially prolonged spinning, with any medical condition (especially a head cold), without adequate sleep or with a hang-over.

Chapter 1

Terminology

Aerobatic flight has its own terminology which isn't quite universal. Let's introduce a few of the common terms.

General Terms

Departure (From Controlled Flight)

Any situation where the flightpath deviates from the direction commanded by the pilot's control input or where the aircraft responds in a manner contrary to the normal, expected response to a particular control input.

Load Factor

The total load or force on the aircraft caused as a result of both gravity and centrifugal reaction – measured in multiples of the force of gravity, or *g*. In scientific papers, load factor may be represented by the symbol Gz.

Rolling *g*

The non-symmetrical load factor experienced by each wing when simultaneously rolling and pitching caused by the aileron deflection in addition to the applied *g*.

Wing-Root Bending Moment

The total bending at the wing-root caused by the total lift force being generated by the particular wing. When pitching, both wing-roots experience the same bending moment. When the aircraft is also rolling, the wing-root bending moment is increased on the wing with the downward deflected aileron as the outboard section of this wing is generating more lift, the centre-of-pressure is displaced further out from the wing-root and therefore causes a greater bending moment. This is why it is dangerous to simultaneously roll wings-level when pulling out of a spiral dive.

Vectors

A vector shows the magnitude and direction of a force or path. Thus the flight-path vector could be a climb at 100 kt or a 3° approach path at 80 kt. The lift vector is always at right angles to the flight-path and the magnitude for our purposes is in multiples of the force gravity (g) – which is the same as multiples of weight.

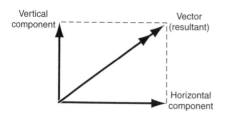

Components

Every force can be resolved into components, either a horizontal and vertical component or perhaps a component along the flightpath and one at 90° to the flightpath.

Resultant

Conversely, several forces can be resolved into one resultant – thus for a turn, gravity and centrifugal reaction can be resolved into a total force which must be overcome by the wings – and in a climb the forces of drag and the component of weight against the direction of the flightpath have to be balanced by the thrust to sustain the climb path angle and speed (vector).

Centripetal Force

Centripetal force is the force that changes the flightpath. The change is in the direction of the applied force. To turn, a force must be applied, towards the centre of the turn. This force, supplied by excess lift from the wings, is called *centripetal* force.

Centrifugal Reaction

To every *action* there is an equal and opposite *reaction*. Thrust is the reaction to the propeller or jet engine pushing air rearwards. Centrifugal reaction is the reaction to centripetal force. It causes the pilot to be pushed into the seat.

Simple Aerobatic Manoeuvres

Rolls

There is no such thing as a simple roll. The following are the common types:

Aileron Roll

A roll nominally about the longitudinal axis of the aircraft, usually a fairly rapid roll and with a straight flightpath. It is normal to raise the nose before beginning the roll so that there is upward momentum to carry the aircraft through the roll without loss of altitude.

Barrel Roll

A combination of rolling, pitching and yawing whereby the aircraft follows a helical flightpath as if it was flying around the inside of a barrel – just like the motorcycle stunt rider inside the horizontal drum.

Slow Roll

A roll around the longitudinal axis while the aircraft follows a nominally straight-and-level flightpath. The roll is deliberately conducted at less than maximum roll rate so that there is a need for deliberate sideslip (knife-edge flight) to maintain altitude with the wings vertical, and a need for deliberate negative angle of attack to maintain the inverted level path. Note that a slow roll does not imply low airspeed.

Hesitation Roll

A roll with distinct pauses – usually at the 90° points (four-point hesitation roll), although some use eight or even more points. The roll-rate is quite rapid to accentuate the pauses. It takes fairly large and rapid control inputs to achieve the distinct and accurate hesitations.

Flick Roll (Snap Roll – US)

An accelerated stall and incipient spin through a half or one turn, sometimes more – usually along a horizontal flightpath, although it is not uncommon in a vertical or 45° up or down direction. It is also used for the half or complete roll at the top of a loop to make a roll-off-the-top or a Porteous loop respectively.

Turns

Chandelle

The chandelle is similar to the first part of the wing-over but is completed at the highest point and lowest speed – the apex of the manoeuvre. It is a means of exchanging airspeed for altitude while changing direction in a small radius. It was the derivation of the Immelman which, in its developed form, is the first half of a loop rather than the first half of a wing-over.

Wing-Over

A gentle pull-up, roll, climbing turn, descending turn, change of direction, through any number of degrees – used to position the aircraft and to establish the entry parameters for the next manoeuvre.

The wing-over is very useful for look-out and for gaining the feel of a new air-craft. Not strictly an aerobatic manoeuvre as all aircraft are capable of a wing-over.

Wing-overs can be joined to form a lazy eight.

Stall Turn (Hammerhead – US)

The stall turn consists of a straight pull-up to the vertical, a pause, a yaw through 180° from vertically upward flight to vertically downward flight and a straight recovery from the vertical dive.

Inverted Turn (Outside Turn)

An inverted or outside turn is made from straight and level inverted flight with the pilot's head outside the flightpath (so there is negative g throughout).

Derry Turn

A roll-under reversal from a steep turn in one direction to a steep turn in the other direction – normally via an aileron roll but sometimes via a flick roll.

Loops

A loop is a manoeuvre entirely in the pitching plane in which the aircraft rotates through 360° in a nominally circular path.

Normal Loop

The normal loop has positive *g* applied throughout and has a nominally constant pitch rate.

Outside Loop

The loop performed with the pilot's head *outside* the flightpath (i.e. negative *g* throughout). It requires an inverted entry and ends inverted. It takes some experience and recent practice to perform.

Square Loop

In a square loop the pitching is conducted in four discreet flightpath changes of 90° with a period of straight flight in between corner. It is a severe manoeuvre requiring rapid *g* application and removal to make the manoeuvre distinct and clearly defined.

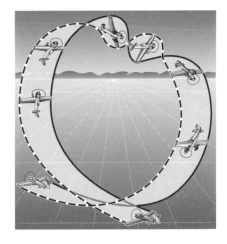

Avalanche (Porteous Loop)

The avalanche (sometimes called the Porteous loop after the Auster test pilot Ranald Porteous) consists of a complete flick roll from inverted flight to inverted flight at the top of the normal loop. It is spectacular yet easy and comfortable to perform.

Complex Aerobatic Manoeuvres

Eights

Horizontal Eight

A three-quarter loop followed by a half roll, a loop from vertically down to vertically down followed by a further half roll and pull out.

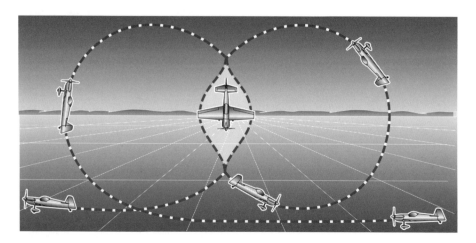

Cuban Eight

A ⅝ loop (through 225° to the 45° downward position) followed by a half roll, a further part loop through 270° (45° down to 45° down), a further half roll and pull-out.

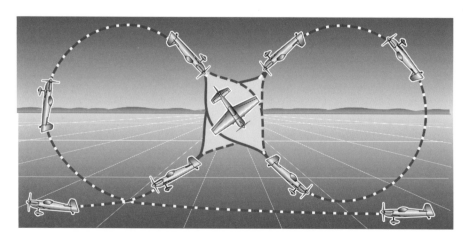

Vertical Eight

A normal loop to inverted with a half roll, loop, further half roll and completion of the first loop.

Clover Leaf

Four loops with 90° downward (or upward) rolls in between.

Roll-Off-the-Top (or Immelmann Turn)

A half loop with a half aileron roll or half flick roll to erect flight at the top. A change in direction in the vertical plane with no horizontal component (developed by WWI pilot Max Immelmann).

Half-Roll-and-Pull-Through (Split-S)

A half aileron roll or half flick roll to inverted flight followed by the downward half of a loop to erect flight.

Vertical S

A half roll, then a downward half loop followed by a further half roll and half loop. The vertical S can equally be performed upwards, as a loop to inverted, half roll, further loop to inverted and a further half roll to erect flight – a half of a vertical eight.

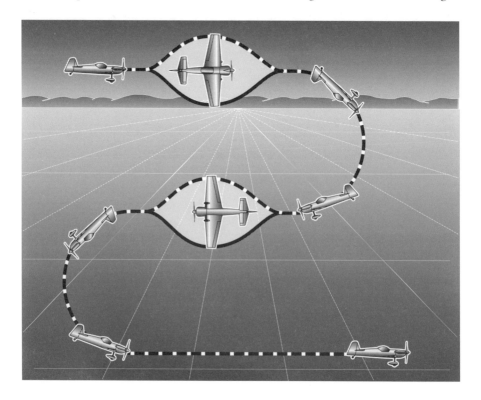

Knife-Edge Flight

A straight-and-level flightpath with the wings vertical. The side-force from the fuselage together with the vertical component of thrust generates the necessary lift.

Sideslip (Also β, Beta)

The lateral (sideways) angle between the longitudinal axis of the fuselage and the relative airflow – in any attitude.

Angle of Attack (Also α, Alpha)

The angle between the chord line of the wing and the free-stream relative airflow.

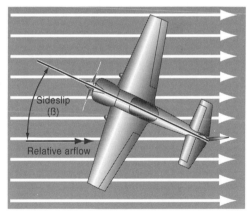

Spins

Spin or Stable Spin

A balance of aerodynamic and gyroscopic (inertia) forces and moments which cause a sustained, low airspeed rotation in yaw, pitch and roll (possibly with some oscillatory motion), and the aircraft following a spiral or helical flightpath with a nominally vertical axis. For an aircraft designed for spinning, this is also a stable spin.

Unstable Spin

A spin where the forces are not balanced – resulting in an oscillation in roll, pitch and/or yaw. Airspeed may fluctuate and eventually increase to a point where one or both wings are unstalled and the aircraft accelerates into a spiral dive.

Flat Spin

A spin whereby the controls are applied to increase the rate of rotation. As a result, the inertia (gyroscopic) forces are enhanced (built up) to cause a higher angle of attack and pitch attitude in the spin (therefore the term, flat spin). The increased rate of rotation usually causes a prolonged recovery time. Some aircraft will not recover from a flat spin. Hence the importance of strictly maintaining the recommended control positions in the spin – as determined for your aircraft type.

Pro-Spin

Any control deflection that maintains the spin, i.e. left aileron in a right spin is both out-spin (opposite to the direction of the spin) and pro-spin as it helps to sustain the spin. (Some aircraft vary.)

Anti-Spin

Against the spin, i.e. left aileron in a left spin is in-spin (in the direction of the spin) and yet anti-spin as it tends to initiate spin recovery.

Inadvertent Inverted Spin

Inverted spins are beyond the scope of most aerobatic trainers and beyond the scope of this book. The inverted spin is simply a departure from controlled inverted flight – either from straight-and-level or turning, during an outside loop or vertical manoeuvre. Be especially careful of rolling to inverted at too slow a speed during a roll-off-the-top when you arrive with *nothing on the clock*. It can also happen as a result of inappropriate control inputs in an erect spin. The aircraft will generally recover if the controls are centralised or released.

Speeds

V_A manoeuvring speed – the speed above which full control deflection is to be avoided. This speed is generally a factored margin above stall speed to ensure that full control deflection will result in a stall before exceeding the structural limits of the airframe. Because it is a factor above stall speed and stall speed varies with all-up-weight then the value of V_A increases with increasing AUW. For a normal-category aircraft with a limit of $+3.8\,g$ then V_A is approximately double V_S. For an aerobatic aircraft V_A may be 2.5 to 3 times V_S.

V_{NO} maximum airspeed, normal operations – the maximum speed for normal flight operations. This speed should only be exceeded, with care, in smooth air.

V_{NE} maximum speed, never exceed – the maximum speed that is not to be exceeded under any circumstances.

V_S the power-off stalling speed clean (flaps and undercarriage up).

Chapter 2

The Physics of Manoeuvring Flight

Isaac In Flight

An aircraft moves in three-dimensions – forwards, backwards, up, down, left and right. Motion in a straight line is called *linear* motion and it may be at constant speed or changing speed. As well as changing speed in a straight line, an aircraft can also change direction – in a temporary or sustained way, and in a sudden or gentle way. The process of changing direction is known as *angular* motion. The motion or rotation takes place around the balance point of the aircraft – known as the *centre of gravity.*

To describe the angular motion, we separate the components into three individual planes or axes. The axes and motions are described as:

- rolling (in the rolling plane) – rotation about the longitudinal axis;
- pitching (in the pitching plane) – rotation about the lateral axis; and
- yawing (in the yawing plane) – rotation about the normal, or vertical, axis.

Some manoeuvres are performed by motion solely in one plane (e.g. a loop is pitching through 360°, an aileron roll is rolling through 360°) or one plane at a time (e.g. stall turn is 90° pitch, followed by yaw through 180°, followed by pitch through 90°). More often a combination of two or three motions is involved (a turn is a combination of pitching and yawing, a barrel roll is rolling and pitching with some yaw, and a spin is yawing, pitching and rolling with perhaps some oscillation).

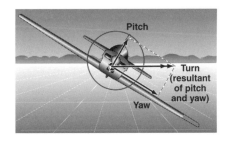

A balanced turn is a combination of pitching and yawing with zero sideslip. However, some manoeuvres may involve deliberate sideslip (e.g. slow roll, knife-edge flight, stall turn and spin) – some of which involve very high sideslip angles.

The Perfect World – No Gravity

Manoeuvring in a zero-*g* world only requires the wings to generate the external reaction to change the flightpath. At zero *g*, zero lift is required to remain airborne. A loop would simply require a set stick position to maintain an angle of attack and the aircraft would fly around the loop at constant speed, constant pitch rate and constant *g*.

A roll would occur around the longitudinal axis of the aircraft at zero angle of attack. No sideslip would be required at the 90° positions and no forward pressure (no negative angle of attack) would be required when inverted.

A turn could be completed with 90° of bank with all lift being used to turn and no component needed to stay aloft. In fact, a turn with less than 90° of bank would result in a climb.

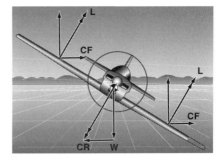

When we add the force of gravity there is a continuing need to generate a force to remain airborne as well as the force to manoeuvre.

If we add gravity and don't correct the rolling manoeuvres, the flightpath curves downward.

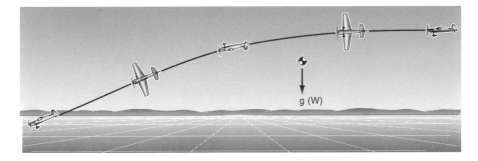

At every stage in any manoeuvre an upward force is required, or the flightpath and/or the speed will change.

For the loop to be round there has to be a changing amount of total *g* so that a constant value of **applied** *g* is maintained. Let's apply +3*g*.

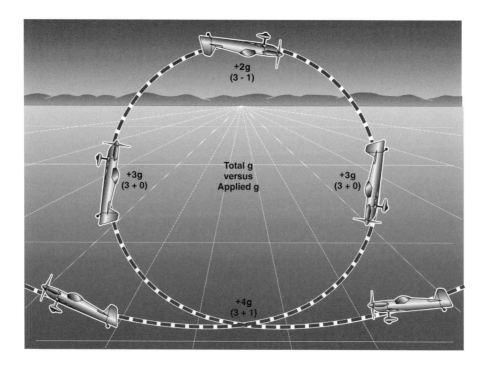

+2g
(3 - 1)

+3g
(3 + 0)

Total g
versus
Applied g

+3g
(3 + 0)

+4g
(3 + 1)

But even then, the speed is going to vary unless the thrust is also varied. And since the amount of thrust is generally limited, there is an inevitable speed variation. Thus the shape of the loop cannot be round unless there is a further adjustment to carry the aircraft over the top.

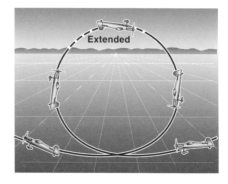

Extended

In the case of the roll, there is a need to sustain an upward force equal to the force of gravity throughout the manoeuvre. Thus there is a positive angle of attack on entry, sideslip at the 90° positions and a negative angle of attack at the inverted position.

The aircraft still rolls around its longitudinal axis but elevator and rudder pressures are required to generate the sideslip and negative angle of attack while the ailerons roll the aircraft.

Many aircraft cannot sustain the level flightpath during this manoeuvre and so it is common to raise the nose and establish an upward flightpath at the beginning of the manoeuvre. The upward momentum allows a slightly curving path which does not leave the aircraft in an unacceptably nose-low attitude and a descending path at the completion of the manoeuvre.

Turning – What Is a Turn?

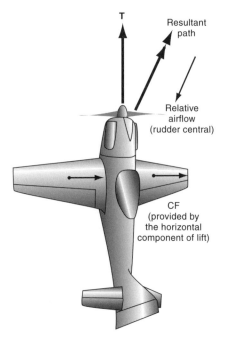

Turning is a combination manoeuvre of pitching and yawing. There is no rolling except on entry and exit. Therefore aileron is not required to maintain the turn (except to balance power effects) unless there is some sideslip to cause a rolling moment. There is no sideslip if the skid ball is centred with the rudder.

So, What Is Causing the Turn?

Pitching is caused by the elevators (back pressure) and this causes the increased angle of attack to generate the excess lift to change the flightpath. The horizontal component of lift provides the centripetal force to change the flightpath.

The yawing component of the turn can be caused by the rudder or by sideslip. That is:

• The turn can be made by banking, applying back pressure and allowing the sideslip to cause the yaw. In this case, the ball will be displaced.

SLIPPING TURN

Pilot slips (falls) into the turn

The ball slips (falls) into the turn

- Alternatively, the rudder can be used to balance. In this case, there is no sideslip and the balance ball is centred.

Hence, even a jet needs the application of some rudder to balance a turn, even though there is no engine torque to be countered. However, a jet has a very large fin and high directional stability, so even a very small amount of sideslip causes the balance in the turn. Thus the ball is very nearly central even when rudder is not applied. Additional rudder may also be needed during the entry and exit to balance any yawing moment caused by aileron deflection (adverse aileron yaw), especially at low airspeeds (high angles of attack).

Which Control Does What?

As the bank angle is increased the ratio of pitching to yawing changes. At 45° of bank there is equal amounts of pitching and yawing.

At 90° of bank there is all pitching and no yawing. A typical steep turn or a maximum rate turn in a light aircraft is performed at 45°–60° of bank, and thus it is mostly pitching, requiring a large amount of back pressure – and very little rudder – to generate the small amount of yawing required.

At these very high angles of bank, most of the available elevator deflection is required to maintain the high angle of attack (close to the critical angle) and pitch rate. If the nose attitude drops, then the amount of extra back pressure to raise the nose is considerable. It is therefore far easier to reduce the bank angle while maintaining the back pressure and therefore the nose will come back up.

Additionally, if the aircraft has insufficient thrust, the only way to maintain best manoeuvring speed is to use gravity to assist, thereby sacrificing altitude for airspeed (potential energy for kinetic energy). In this case, again, with the wing close to the critical angle of attack, the pilot holds the back pressure constant and *plays* the bank angle to raise and lower the nose attitude to maintain airspeed.

Attitude, Angle of Attack and Flightpath

It is important before analysing the aerobatic manoeuvres that we distinguish some terms and understand some significant elements. It is vital to distinguish between the terms *attitude, flightpath* and *angle of attack.*

The *attitude* of the aircraft is the position of the nose in relation to the horizon.

This aircraft has a:
• level attitude; with a
• descending flightpath.

The *flightpath* of the aircraft is the direction it is travelling relative to the horizon.

This aircraft has a:
• level flightpath; but
• a nose-high attitude.

The *angle of attack* is the angle of the wing to the relative airflow.

This aircraft has the same angle of attack, but also a:
• climbing flightpath; and
• a very nose-high attitude.

Note: Each of the aircraft shown has the *same angle of attack* (the same IAS but varying thrust), an increasing pitch attitude and a descending, level and climbing flightpath respectively.

The *attitude* of the aircraft is where it is *pointing* (as distinct from where it is *going*).

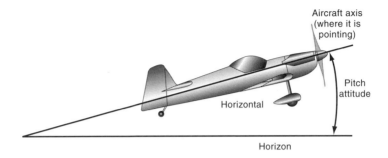

The *flightpath* is where it is going and this can be referenced to the airflow, the horizon (as is usual), or relative to a point on the the ground, a runway or display line (for approach and landing or for display aerobatics respectively). This latter path also takes into account the effects of wind. The difference between these references, although subtle, is very significant.

Airspeed is speed through the air. *Groundspeed* is speed relative to the earth and therefore includes the effects of wind. Speed relative to the earth is the measure of absolute speed. Groundspeed determines the *momentum* and the *kinetic energy* of the aircraft.

The only way to adjust the flightpath to reach a point on the ground, against the wind, is to increase the thrust. *Thrust* is the means to overcome drag (plus gravity in some situations) and headwind. Thrust *sustains* the flightpath.

How Does an Aircraft Manoeuvre?

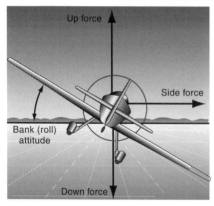

Any change of speed or direction is caused by generating an additional force in the direction the pilot wishes the aircraft to go.

Newton correctly observed that:
- a body will continue in its state of rest or uniform motion in a straight line, unless acted upon by an external force; and
- the rate of change of momentum is proportional to the applied force and takes place in the direction in which the force acts, i.e. the direction and speed will change in the direction it is pushed and the rate of change is proportional to the amount of push.

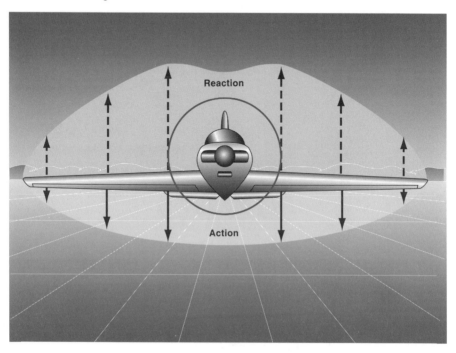

The pilot can cause the aircraft to accelerate or decelerate by changing thrust, or by using gravity (by diving or climbing) – but the only way to change the direction of the flightpath is to generate an external force in the required direction. In the absence of vectored thrust, the pilot can only use excess lift from the wings to push the air and cause a reaction in the direction he wishes to go. So the potential to generate excess lift is the potential to manoeuvre.

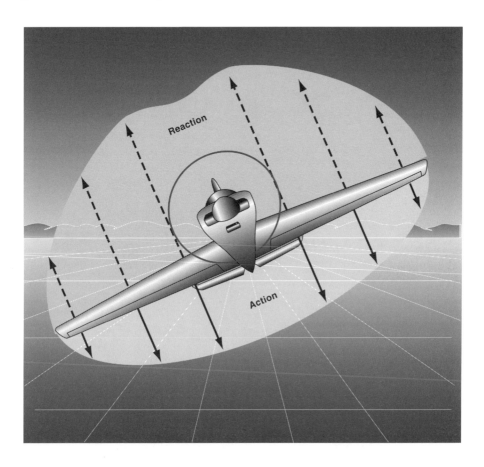

Note: *excess* lift – if there is no excess over that required to stay airborne, then there is no force available to change direction. When flying at V_S you cannot maintain level flight and also turn. There is some misunderstanding that the minimum-radius turn occurs at the slowest speed. In practice, it does not and it cannot. It occurs at the critical angle of attack and is at its minimum when the critical angle is reached at the limiting load factor. At V_S you have no manoeuvre potential – none, *zero*.

The ability to manoeuvre depends on airspeed above the stall (more correctly the angle of attack margin below the critical angle). At any speed, the pilot can apply elevator deflection to the point when the critical angle is reached and beyond which the wing will stall. At very low speed the wing is already close to the critical angle and so the potential for excess lift is low. At higher speed, the angle of attack is low and the margin to the critical angle is great – so there is plenty of potential excess lift available to manoeuvre. The limit then becomes one of available thrust or the structural limits of the airframe.

At V_A the critical angle is nominally reached at the point when the positive load factor limit is also achieved, e.g. at twice the stalling speed the pilot can apply +4g and no more. For an aircraft to be able to reach a maximum limit of say, +9g, the airspeed has to be at or above $3 \times V_S$. Below this speed, the wing will reach the critical angle of attack, i.e. it will stall, before being able to reach the structural g-limit.

Zooms, Climbs and Dives

You will be familiar with terms like *climb, dive, zoom* and *roll*, but now we need to be more specific about their precise meanings, so that we can understand what is happening to the aircraft. Any aircraft can follow almost any flightpath for a moment or two. If we accelerate a Jumbo to its maximum speed we could gently pull up to a very steep angle. We would be gaining altitude but we would not be climbing because we would not be able to sustain the climbing path. The airspeed would be falling – rapidly. This temporary exchange of airspeed for altitude is called a *zoom*.

In the opposite case, a descent or glide can be sustained and the speed controlled. A *dive*, however, is a descending flightpath where the speed is increasing.

Thus when we are manoeuvring, we are using a combination of both temporary and sustainable manoeuvres to position the aircraft, but it is the sustained manoeuvres (a function of the aircraft's excess thrust) that ultimately allow us to perform a sequence of aerobatics within a specified altitude band.

The Nature of Manoeuvring

The Laws

Maximum Performance Manoeuvring (Flight at the Limits)

It is one thing to pull suddenly on the control column to reach $+6g$, but it's an entirely different matter to be able to sustain a load factor of $+6g$. What limits us?

The ability of an aircraft to manoeuvre is ultimately limited by:
- excess (spare) lift;
- excess (spare) thrust; and
- structural strength.

The relevant limit depends on the actual flight condition at the time, e.g. above or below V_A, light or heavy weight and flap and undercarriage configuration.

Additionally, the human pilot may impose limits on the manoeuvre capability of the aircraft because of physiological limits or lack of training and recent practice. This is an important and wise precaution – too often ignored.

To manoeuvre, i.e. to change the flightpath in a particular direction, requires a force to be generated in that direction. The pilot has four forces at his disposal and thus four forces by which the flightpath can be changed. They are thrust, weight, drag and lift. The most powerful force available to the pilot is the lift force, and the pilot has the means to direct this force by banking and to control the amount of lift by changing the angle of attack.

To change direction the pilot needs to create a force towards the centre of the manoeuvre. *Centripetal force* is equivalent to the piece of string that you need to rotate a stone around your head. Without the string, the stone departs in a straight line.

An aircraft is the same.

- To accelerate forwards, we can increase thrust or we can dive and use the force of gravity.
- To climb, we can increase thrust or change flightpath by increasing lift momentarily and then use momentum to carry the aircraft a limited vertical distance.
- To decelerate, we can either reduce thrust, increase drag (with speed brakes or undercarriage extension) or raise the nose and use gravity to slow us down.
- To change the direction of the flightpath sideways, we can bank and use part of the lift force (a component of the lift force) to generate the centripetal force to cause the turn while maintaining a vertical component to balance the force of gravity.
- To loop, we use the excess lift to generate centripetal force to change the flightpath continuously around the manoeuvre.

A simple roll (aileron roll or slow roll) does not need a centripetal force as the flightpath does not need to be changed. All that is needed is a rolling moment (a twisting force caused by the ailerons) while the aircraft proceeds along its original flightpath. However this is not the case for the barrel roll. The barrel roll does have a changing flightpath around a spiral and both rolling and pitching moments, as well as centripetal force, are needed. There is a need for a rolling moment from the ailerons and a pitching moment from the elevators – and there is a need for a sustained centripetal force towards the central axis of the barrel.

For a loop, the aircraft uses momentum from the dive to sustain the initial climbing path and maximum thrust to offset the induced drag and the force of gravity – to allay the airspeed reduction. Over the top, gravity will help the flightpath change and only a small centripetal force is needed. On the downside, drag is needed to contain the acceleration, and thrust reduction, speed brakes and induced drag (pulling harder) can be used for this purpose.

An aircraft with sufficient excess thrust (more thrust than weight and induced drag combined) can pull up and sustain the looping manoeuvre from any speed – but this is exceptional.

Energy

Aircraft with limited thrust can compensate by use of other means to allow a limited manoeuvre potential that is beyond its normal capability. Stored energy in the form of spare altitude over your minimum (*potential energy*) or spare airspeed over V_s (*kinetic energy*) provides you with the capacity to manoeuvre. It's like having a credit rating or money in the bank.

Zoom potential is money in the bank to be used when needed. Spare altitude gives potential energy which can be converted into speed and spare speed can be converted into altitude. Thus, don't ever be low and slow – especially in an aircraft without much excess thrust. You have nowhere to go; no reserves to play with. If you are low and have excess speed you have excess lift (to turn) or momentum (*zoom potential*) to climb.

See how people become trapped in valleys. They are low already and then they slow down to allow more reaction time or in the belief that they can manoeuvre better (more tightly) at a lower speed. But then they have the capacity neither to manoeuvre nor to zoom – no ability to turn or to zoom over a hill, even into cloud at an angle higher than the rising terrain. At low speed, the induced drag is already high, they are closer to the stalling angle with little excess lift available and they are in an aircraft without much excess thrust. It's nowhere to be and there's nowhere to go.

A motor vehicle can turn at very slow speed because it is sitting on the ground, and it doesn't need to generate lift. It is limited at higher speeds because there is a loss of tyre friction to generate the high centripetal force required (i.e. it will skid). This is not the same as the aircraft. The very best turn that an aircraft can perform is at a speed where the wing reaches its critical angle of attack at the maximum allowable load factor. For a training aircraft (non-aerobatic), this is approximately twice the stalling speed. There is no value in being slower than this. Whether this turn can be sustained in level flight is a matter of excess thrust, but in this situation a 180° turn is the most we need and perhaps we can sacrifice a little spare altitude (if we kept any).

We've mentioned Newton's law of motion and how the wing generates excess lift to cause the flightpath of the fuselage and its occupants to be changed. We'll now examine the control of that lifting force and its effects on the structure of the aircraft. The aircraft's ability to change the flightpath and speed depends on the ability of excess lift and excess thrust. Conversely, the aircraft's performance limits are determined by its manoeuvre potential, again excess lift and excess thrust until, of course, we reach either the structural limits of the aircraft, the airspeed limits or the pilot's limit. Lets look at these in turn.

Excess (Spare) Lift

In straight-and-level flight, lift equals weight. If we are flying close to the stalling speed, the wing is close to its stalling angle and therefore there is not much spare capacity to generate additional lift. The margin to the stall is small, therefore the aircraft's ability to manoeuvre at speeds close to the stalling is extremely limited.

If we are in straight-and-level flight, at twice the aircraft's stalling speed, the wings are capable of generating four times the amount of lift that they can generate at the stalling speed. If it needs one magnitude of lift to balance the weight, then there are three spare amounts of lift with which we can manoeuvre the aircraft. Its manoeuvre potential is a total of 4g. If we are flying at three times the aircraft's stalling speed, the amount of lift that can be generated is nine times the weight, or 9g. Therefore, our manoeuvre potential, at any particular time, is determined by our excess airspeed, that is the margin above the stalling speed. This excess lift determines our capability to instantaneously change the flightpath of the aircraft. To sustain a changing flightpath, we also have to take into account induced drag and therefore our ability to counter that drag; thus the next factor that determines our manoeuvre potential is the amount of available excess thrust.

Excess (Spare) Thrust

The high angle of attack necessary to generate 6*g* brings with it induced drag. The ability to sustain a manoeuvre depends on the excess thrust available and also the direction of the manoeuvre in relation to the force of gravity. Yes, gravity is still there.

In a level turn at 6*g*, gravity is part of the total force that the wings have to overcome – the wings are countering gravity and generating a centripetal force to change the flightpath. At the bottom of a loop, gravity also adds to the required force needed to change the flightpath, whereas at the top of a loop, gravity helps. This is why the First World War fighters used the Immelmann turn (roll-off-the-top); they fought gravity at the beginning when they had excess speed and used gravity to help them at the top when they had little excess.

We know that the aircraft's angle of climb is proportional to its excess thrust. Having overcome drag, the amount of spare thrust determines how steeply we can climb. When we are manoeuvering an aircraft, we are increasing the angle of attack of the wing. When we increase the angle of attack of the wing, we generate induced drag – a drag that is induced as a result of making lift.

The amount of induced drag is dependent on angle of attack, but also for a given design, it depends on aspect ratio (actually the spanwise distribution of lift or weight in relation to span) and to a lesser extent, the shape or planform of the wing. Thus a highly loaded stubby wing with square tips has very high induced drag. A biplane may have even more.

You will know the shape of the Spitfire with its elliptical wing planform.

An elliptical wing is more complex and more expensive to manufacture than a wing with a constant section, because all of the ribs are different and you have compound curves. However, the benefit in flight is significant. The almost perfect spanwise distribution of lift combined with the small wingtips reduces induced drag. This means that the aircraft can manoeuvre without substantial loss of performance.

Conversely, an aircraft with straight, constant section wings has a very high induced drag. It may be fast but it slows when it turns. A small aerobatic training aircraft generally has to climb to altitude before manoeuvring and loses altitude throughout an aerobatic sequence, even with the use of full power.

The significance of this induced drag is illustrated by the Avions Mudry CAP 10 with its elliptical wing. Although relatively low-powered, it can complete an aerobatic sequence without loss of altitude and, if managed properly, can even climb throughout.

Structural Limits

As we have seen, to manoeuvre the aircraft, the pilot increases the angle of attack of the wing and the wings apply a force to change the direction of the fuselage. This force is transmitted through the point of attachment of the wings and is felt as a force which also tries to bend the wing. This is called the wing-root bending moment.

Incidentally, a flying wing has no wing-root bending moment because the load is spread over the wing rather than concentrated in the fuselage and thus can have a much lighter structure and withstand the same high loads.

The ability of the structure to withstand the g forces is primarily dependent on two factors:
- The ability of the wing-root and any additional struts or bracing wires to absorb the wing-root bending moment, and

- The strength of the tailplane (for vertical loads) and the fin (for side-loads).

An aerobatic training aircraft is designed to allow the pilot to apply +6*g* and −3*g*. (An aircraft in the utility category approved for limited manoeuvring may be designed to +4.5*g* and −1.5*g*.)

Both the tailplane and the wing-root are designed to allow these loads to be reached as an everyday occurrence without permanent deformation nor structural damage. The fin and rudder also have to be able to withstand the high side loads associated with knife-edge flight and flick manoeuvres (if approved).

Another consideration is the ability of the control surfaces and trim tabs to withstand tail-slides − something for which many aircraft are not designed − and therefore such manoeuvres are prohibited.

To provide a safety margin, the structure is in fact designed to and tested to at least 1.5 times this value. While the structure may suffer some damage or permanent deformation, the structure must not suffer failure unless 1.5 times + 6 or 1.5 times − 3 (i.e. +9*g* or −4.5*g*) is exceeded, even for a short time. The reason for this margin is to allow the pilot to fly to the published limits and to keep a reserve of structural strength in the event that he flies through turbulence, or applies additional control deflections which cause the loading to be non-symmetrical. However, above the normal limit some damage may occur and it may be expensive to repair.

Think about the loads that the engine mounts are having to carry also!

Rolling *g*

Imagine an aircraft pulling out of a straight dive and the pilot applying +6*g*. Each wing is trying to bend upwards from its root. Because it's a straight dive, each wing is generating the same amount of lift and each wing-root is experiencing the same bending moment.

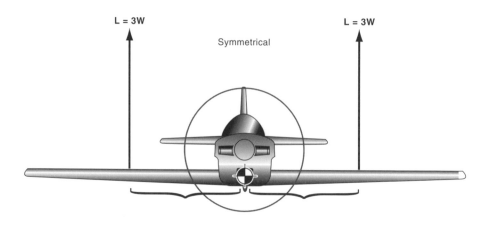

L = 3W   L = 3W

Symmetrical

If at the same time as applying the +6*g* the pilot now applies full aileron deflection, the change in camber and therefore the amount of lift generated by each wing is changed.

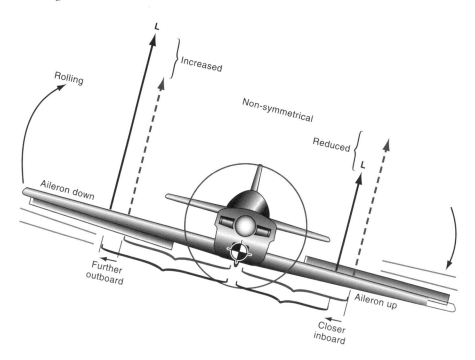

The wing that has the aileron deflected downwards is generating more lift than the symmetrical case, and not only that, the centre of the lifting force is further outboard on the wing because the outboard section is doing more of the work. It has a higher angle of attack or greater camber. Therefore, that wing and that wingroot are experiencing a bending moment beyond the +6*g* of the symmetrical pullout. The other wing, with the aileron deflected upwards, has a reduced amount of lift and the centre of lift is moved inboard because the outer part of the wing is doing less work. Therefore, its wing-root bending moment is considerably reduced.

This imbalance in load factor due to aileron deflection is called 'rolling *g*', and there is no indication of it in the cockpit. So, to ensure that we don't exceed our normal +6*g* limit, the pilot must reduce the load factor whenever he wants to simultaneously apply aileron deflection. As a guide, the pilot should not apply full aileron deflection if the aircraft is experiencing a load factor in excess of two-thirds of the limit for symmetrical flight. That is, if the aircraft is designed to a pilot limit of +6*g* symmetrical, the pilot should only apply full aileron deflection during manoeuvres at load factors below +4*g*. This allowance also applies to negative rolling-*g* manoeuvres.

Spades

The development of fighters in World War II allowed higher and higher airspeeds to the extent that control forces became excessive. The size of the aileron surface needed to provide high rates-of-roll was causing very high control loads. Spades were developed to allow the large surface but to reduce the control force. They acted as an aerodynamic balance. They were successful, but soon after, powered control systems were developed and the spades disappeared. They have been reintroduced in several competition aerobatic aircraft.

Gusts

An aircraft which flies through a changing current of air will momentarily feel the added gust as an increase or reduction in applied g depending on the orientation of the gust. If the aircraft is pulling up for a roll-off-the-top at $+6g$ and flies through a thermal with a strong vertically upward current, then the aircraft will be over-stressed. The aircraft will have another speed known as turbulence penetration speed, or V_B, which is the recommended speed for flight in turbulence. An aircraft that is being manoeuvred in such an atmosphere should be flown at a safe margin below the g limits. An aircraft at the critical angle of attack and at high g that flies through a vertical gust could experience an accelerated stall and departure. Any applied load is additive – that is to say that any load due to gravity, to manoeuvring or to turbulence adds up to the point where the aircraft could either stall (below V_A) or be overstressed. This applies to both symmetrical flight and to rolling g. Neither an accelerated stall nor overstress is acceptable in aerobatic flight and so the only protection is for the pilot to leave a margin of g or angle of attack below the limits. When manoeuvring in turbulent air or when there is a possibility of vertical gusts or windshear, then the pilot should stay within two-thirds of allowable limits.

Pilot Limits

There are absolute limits beyond which damage will occur, and there are pilot limits. Don't be confused. There are two *pilot* limits:
- factored structural limits to which the pilot can routinely fly, while maintaining a safety margin below absolute structural limits; and
- the pilot's personal physiological limits (these are discussed in the next chapter).

Flight Envelope

We mentioned that the ability of an aircraft to manoeuvre is limited by:
- the amount of excess lift it can generate;
- the amount of excess thrust; and
- the structural limits (aircraft or pilot!).

Provided we have excess speed above the stall, we have excess lift available to us, but at any speed, that lift is limited by the fact that the wing will ultimately reach its stalling angle or critical angle of attack. At any time during manoeuvring flight, the pilot has enough control power to increase the angle of attack of the wing to its stalling angle (provided it is loaded within normal limits). It will then either reach the structural limit of the aircraft (at speeds above V_A), or at lower speeds it will reach the stalling angle, beyond which it rapidly loses its lifting capability. For each aircraft, there is a published flight envelope, and for some this is generally portrayed in what is called a V-n diagram.

The V-n Diagram

The V-n diagram shows the flight envelope of the aircraft in terms of its minimum speeds, its maximum speeds, its maximum load factors (positive and negative) and where in the envelope the limit occurs. If you look at the diagram, you will see the upper structural limit defines the line across the top of the envelope, the limiting speed defines the right hand boundary, the limiting structural strength for negative g determines the lower boundary, and the converging lines on the left–hand edge are dictated by the wing reaching its positive, or negative, stalling angle of attack.

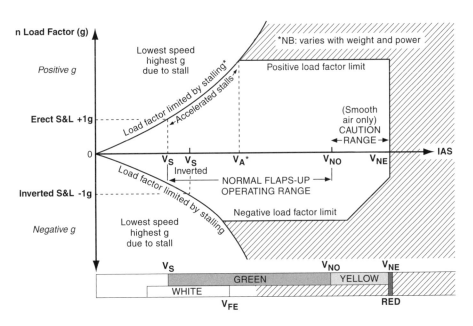

Thus, for each speed, there is a corresponding limit, which below the corner point is determined by stall, and above it by structural restrictions. This corner point represents a speed known as manoeuvring, or V_A. It is the speed below which the pilot can apply full control deflection without exceeding the structural limit of the aircraft.

That is to say, it is the point where the aircraft will stall before it will reach the limiting load factor. It is vital to know the V_A speed for your aircraft. Note that it is based on the clean, power-off stalling speed and therefore varies with configuration, power and AUW. Your aircraft may have a range of values for V_A for different weights.

Load Factor Limits

In the training aircraft you've flown previously, you would have felt small amounts of g during steep turns, perhaps as much as $+2g$ if you did a 60° banked level turn. For aerobatic manoeuvring, you will regularly experience $+4g$, perhaps a little more. Aerobatic aircraft should be fitted with an additional instrument to show exactly what load factor the aircraft is experiencing.

The g meter, or accelerometer, simply has a small bob-weight on a spring. The more the aircraft manoeuvres, the more the spring is stretched, and the more the needle is deflected. It shows both positive and negative g and, as well as the moveable needle, has two tell-tale needles which are deflected to show, at the end of the flight, the maximum positive and negative g reached during that flight. These needles are resettable for each flight. If you get into an aircraft and any of the needles show an amount of g in excess of the normal limits, then don't take that aircraft – have it checked.

It is wise for aerobatic training aircraft to have two g meters, one of which cannot be reset except by the maintenance engineers. That way any overstress is recorded and inspected before the meter is reset and the aircraft flies again. There are now electronic flight recorders available that record the loads and the number of applications. These are a wonderful development for managing the safe use of aerobatic aircraft.

Obviously, an aerobatic training aircraft needs to be able to sustain flight loads that can be expected in normal aerobatic manoeuvres – and it must have a reserve for safety. For an aerobatic aircraft, the structure is required to withstand a pilot limit (what the pilot is *allowed* to apply – as distinct from what the pilot can *tolerate*) of $+6g$ and $-3g$, i.e. there must be no permanent damage or deformation of the structure unless $+6g$ or $-3g$ is exceeded. A 1.5 safety margin then ensures that no catastrophic failure occurs unless $+9g$ or $-4.5g$ are exceeded. This is called the ultimate load factor limit. Rolling g limits are two-thirds of these. A competition aerobatic aircraft could have ultimate limits of perhaps $\pm12g$.

An aircraft in the utility category (FAR 23) will have a limit of $+4.5g$ and -1.5 with the same 1.5 margin. Some aircraft may be both normal or utility category depending on the number of persons, fuel and baggage. It is vital to observe the particular limits (weight and CG) for the utility category, before the aircraft is manoeuvred or spun. Be particularly careful to observe weight and CG limits for smaller aircraft such as the Cessna 150/152 or Tomahawk.

Manoeuvring Efficiently Within the Limits

Let us consider the V-n diagram and the boundaries that it offers. When the wing approaches the stalling angle, we can generate no further lift and therefore the aircraft is said to be lift-limited or we've reached the lift boundary. To sustain manoeuvering flight, for example a level steep turn, we have to increase thrust to match the induced drag, otherwise the airspeed will decay during the turn. If the aircraft has sufficient excess thrust to maintain airspeed at that particular value of *g*, then the aircraft could continue there all day – no loss of speed, no loss of altitude. However, only the high-performance aircraft, such as the competition aerobatic aeroplanes, or combat aircraft, have this amount of excess thrust.

For most aircraft, the ability to sustain a manoeuvre is limited by excess thrust, and this forms the thrust boundary. For example, an aircraft that has a low aspect ratio generates a massive wing-tip vortex and therefore very high values of induced drag. Delta-winged aircraft, such as the Mirage, even on full afterburner (reheat), could not maintain a level turn on the buffet, without losing performance. Despite the high thrust available, the airspeed would decay because of the enormous induced drag at high angles of attack.

The only way aircraft can maintain a turn under these circumstances is to lower the nose and use gravity to maintain airspeed – thereby sacrificing altitude (potential energy) for airspeed (kinetic energy).

Conversely, the pilot is able to exchange airspeed for altitude. So if the aircraft is flying along at three times its stalling speed, it can apply $+9g$ instantaneously or it can zoom, perhaps to several thousand feet. This is what energy management is all about. The finesse of aerobatic flying is to manage the energy during the sequence so that the aircraft completes the sequence with the expected level of energy, i.e. the best speed and altitude, perhaps even the same level of energy as it began. Most aircraft are not capable of doing this and one generally has to begin manoeuvring with an excess of energy to be able to complete the sequence at a safe speed and altitude.

Pilots of single-engined, propeller-driven aircraft, especially with short wingspan and high power (the aircraft, not the pilot), also have to take into account the gyroscopic forces and torque reaction due to the engine and propeller rotation. Manoeuvres will be considerably easier in one direction than the other and piloting technique may have to be modified for manoeuvres in the opposite direction.

The Roller-Coaster and Centripetal Force

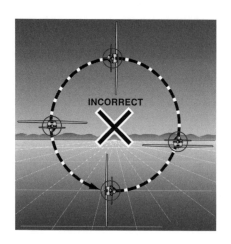

Now to the barrel roll. It is a special case because it is deceptively easy and because it is still largely misunderstood. It has killed many display pilots. Many texts on aerobatics show the highest point of the barrel roll being when the wings are vertical, and that the aircraft passes the wings-level, inverted position when the aircraft is passing the entry level on the downside. Some even say that the aircraft should be pointing at the reference point when the aircraft passes the wings vertical position.

None of this is correct. Gravity won't allow it and not even Mr Newton could fly it. The ultimate result must be to fall out of the bottom of the manoeuvre.

If you have books showing the barrel roll this way, be careful. It is a dangerous misconception and has been the probable cause of several air-display accidents. Display pilots and formation leaders, believing this technique, have **pulled** the nose down after the wings-vertical position. This virtually ensured that there was insufficient altitude to complete the roll, and in the case of low-altitude display flying, inevitably led to the aircraft hitting the ground.

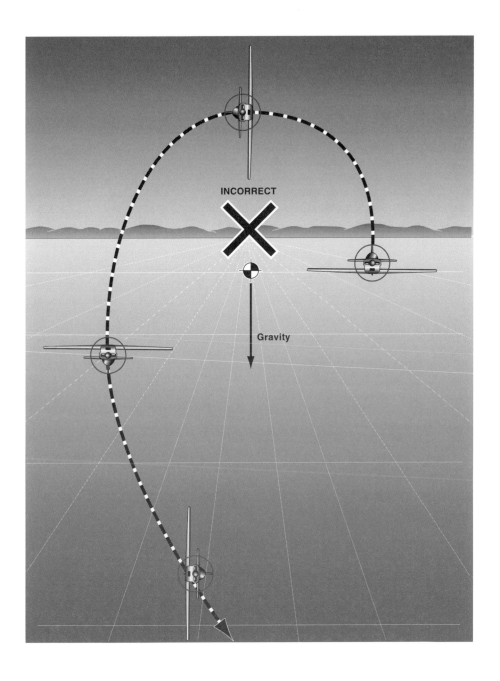

If the pilot tries to follow the simplistic view of the roll, there is great danger that it will be impossible to prevent the rapidly descending path through the second half of the roll. Unless the aircraft is capable of a much higher roll-rate, the pilot may not be able to recover before ground impact.

Inverted Dive

There is a further insidious effect of the nose-down inverted position during the second half of the barrel roll, or indeed during the inverted, speed-increasing part of any manoeuvre. Natural stability of the aircraft causes the nose to pitch-up with increasing airspeed. In erect flight this has the effect of containing the airspeed and restoring the status quo. If the aircraft is inverted and accelerating then the stability is now pitching the nose up with respect to the pilot's view but down with respect to the earth. Thus the dive steepens and the aircraft will not assist recovery. Only the pilot can change the trend by rolling upright or applying negative *g*.

You may have read about the *victory roll* performed by fighter pilots as they returned from a successful mission with a *kill*. They would join the circuit and then perform the roll. So many died from this manoeuvre that it was eventually banned – as was the *garbage roll* after take-off with the undercarriage and flaps down. It was a terrible waste of life – because the pilots did not understand the nature of the rolling manoeuvre and the danger of the nose being low at the half-way point. Remember that the war-time pilots were relatively inexperienced.

From basic science, we know that there must be a force towards the centre of the roll. This is centripetal force and it can only be generated by the wings as excess lift. (Sideforce from the fuselage and fin is relatively small and the sideslip angles would have to be high.) Thus the only practicable way the aircraft can follow the spiral path of the barrel roll is by the wing force being directed towards the central axis of the roll.

There is no other way. Designers of roller-coasters know this so that they don't have the passengers falling-out during the roll.

It is true that the nose-up pitch attitude is highest at the wings-vertical position, but the aircraft still has an upward flightpath due to momentum and it reaches the highest point in the manoeuvre at the wings-level inverted position.

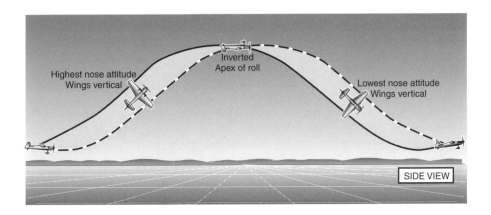

The importance of this relationship between attitude, flightpath and apogee (the highest point of the manoeuvre) is significant.

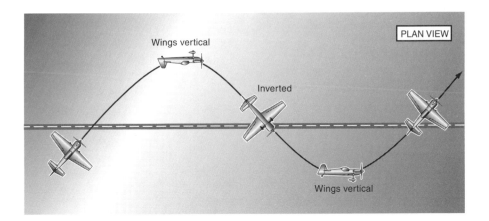

In fact, it is the same as all manoeuvres, including the loop.

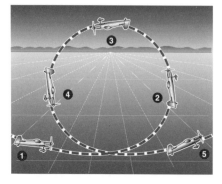

The highest point is half way and the steepest nose-up and nose-down attitudes are at the ¼ and ¾ positions.

Let's re-examine the aircraft's attitude at different points of the barrel roll and also see where the aircraft is located in the flightpath. See how the highest nose *attitude* is not the highest point, not the highest *altitude*.

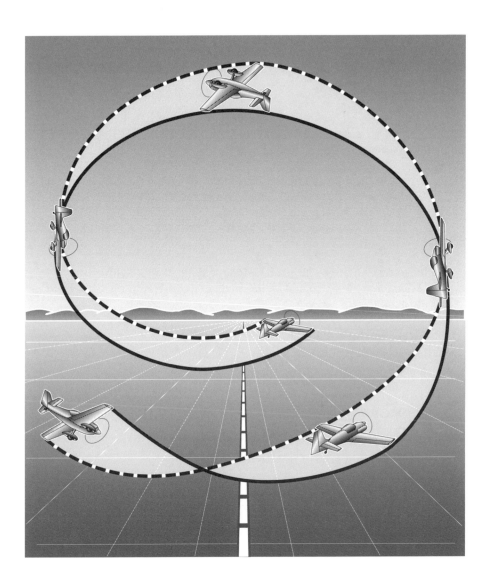

Low-Speed Flight

To understand manoeuvring flight, we have to change our personal attitude and ingrained association between airspeed and angle of attack. In straight-and-level flight, there is a close relationship. However, in manoeuvring flight there is none. We can be at high speed and stall. We can be well below the stalling speed and nowhere near the stalling angle. Angle of attack is determined by stick position – at any speed. Airspeed affects only the power of the controls and the influence of the stabilising surfaces.

Stalling

We will begin in straight-and-level flight at low speed. The angle of attack is high, the ailerons are sloppy and the power will be fairly high to overcome the induced drag.

We have seen the control column has the power to stall the wing at any speed (except perhaps at the forward CG limit), and at speeds below V_A there is no risk of exceeding the structural limits.

To be able to anticipate the stall, we need now to reconsider our previous training.

No longer will an impending stall be indicated by:
- a nose-high attitude (we could be inverted, nose-down with full power and still stall the wing);
- sloppy controls (could stall at any speed);
- quiet (any power setting); and
- airspeed (it can stall at any speed).

What do we have left?

The reliable cues are:
- stall warning horn or light (OK, because it is based on angle of attack);
- buffet (also based on angle of attack);
- stick force (provided we haven't re-trimmed); and
- stick position (if the CG is correct).

If the elevators are greatly deflected, the angle of attack is high – no matter what attitude, speed or power setting.

So we stall by pulling back on the control column and we un-stall by releasing that back pressure. It's as simple as that. Negative stalls are caused by pushing on the control column and are avoided by releasing the forward pressure. Once again, leaving the trim set for high-speed cruise improves the feel and the warning we have of how close we are to the stalling angle. If we trim out the force there is less pull force, and so less warning.

Loss and Restoration of Controlled Flight

The terms, *stall, incipient spin, incipient stall, accelerated stall, autorotation, region of reversed command, post-stall gyrations,* and *spin* are well encompassed by the American definition, *departure from controlled flight.* This expression was coined to describe any situation where the aircraft did not do what the pilot wanted or did what the pilot didn't want – i.e. it behaved in a manner not in accordance with normal expectations to the control inputs that were applied, a manner to which we are not accustomed.

Generally, one wing, or a significant part of one wing, has exceeded the stalling angle, and depending on the particular aircraft, we can expect uncommanded rolling, yawing and pitching deviations from controlled flight.

Several aspects are consistent, though. We have to be at or close to the stalling angle. There has to be a control input, sideslip, roll-rate, yawing moment, torque, slipstream or gust that causes one wing to go *over the edge.* Any subsequent attempt by the pilot to restore the flightpath by conventional control inputs can aggravate the situation and actually cause the reverse of what is required, e.g. using aileron to pick up a stalled wing will cause it to deviate further and faster. Thus the response is *uncommanded.* The aircraft *autorotates.*

As well as the change in angle of attack due to the deflected ailerons, the presence of adverse aileron yaw can cause a yawing moment which itself will accentuate any departure tendency.

The simple solution in all cases is to take both wings clear of the stall by reducing the angle of attack. Then all controls will once again respond conventionally.

Stop the yaw and stop the sideslip. There will be no spin. Reduce the angle of attack. There will be no stall.

Any dynamics that have developed will disappear after a few oscillations, once the angle of attack is reduced. If it all happened in a vertically upward flightpath, then holding the reduced angle of attack and allowing the aircraft to accelerate into a nose-down path will see order restored.

Departure from Controlled Flight

Avoiding Loss of Control

If back pressure is partially released as soon as the aerodynamic buffet or the stall warning is evident then there will be no loss of normal control response. In any attitude and at any speed, the wing cannot and will not stall without being forced to. Even exceeding the stalling angle will not result in a departure unless there is an imbalance, sideslip or applied power, and even then the rudder will be effective in preventing any uncommanded roll or yaw.

Regaining Control

In almost every case, control is immediately restored as soon as the angle of attack is reduced below the stalling angle for both wings. Any build-up of gyroscopic forces can then be countered in a conventional way.

Autorotation

You will recall your theory lessons about autorotation and spinning. As the aircraft departs from controlled flight, the pro-spin forces and moments cause the aircraft to gyrate in yaw, roll and pitch. The rate of rotation builds until gyroscopic forces and moments come into play. For a deliberate spin, the pilot's control inputs (full rudder and full back stick) over-ride the aircraft's natural stability and tendency to recover unaided. The aerodynamic forces are subdued and the rotation accelerates. Centralising the controls is generally sufficient to prevent a spin from developing.

In early aircraft designs, the aircraft could stall asymmetrically simply due to aileron deflection at the stall. Newer designs won't depart unless gross control inputs are applied, and even then most also require deliberate rudder deflection.

Some aircraft have a tendency, or a greater tendency, to depart if they are stalled with power applied and, perhaps, with flaps extended.

Spinning

The spin is ultimately a vertically downward flightpath at low airspeed during which the aircraft yaws, rolls and pitches fairly rapidly in a helical path around a vertical axis. In the developed (stabilised) spin, everything builds to a situation where the aerodynamic forces and moments trying to counter the spin are balanced by the gyroscopic forces and moments trying to continue the spin – and all equals all. Gravity ensures that the flightpath is ultimately downwards.

For aerobatic manoeuvring, a prolonged spin is not very useful as it consumes energy – the altitude loss does not result in zoom potential as the airspeed remains low. So, other than using it to change direction or lose altitude in a spectacular way, there is no point staying beyond one or one-and-a-half turns. Further, the physiological consequences of spinning beyond 4 or 5 turns can be adverse. There is an deceptive effect on the pilot's vestibular apparatus (balance mechanism) after 4–5 rotations whereby recovery from a spin in one direction can be perceived as the entry to a spin in the opposite direction.

Historically, there are stories of almost every aircraft type having had accidents due to prolonged spinning – even after they have been in service for many years. The Tiger Moth had strakes added. The Chipmunk had to undergo extensive trials to discover why it was sometimes very difficult to recover from prolonged spins. It, too, adopted strakes. The Robin 2160 received a ventral fin. The Bulldog and Firefly have had some unexplained situations. The Cessna Aerobat and Piper Tomahawk have had spinning accidents which also have not been fully explained.

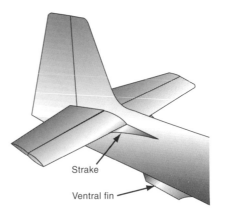

Strake

Ventral fin

All of these types are spun very frequently and it may be unfair to highlight what are only occasional problems. However, it seems that prolonged spins allow the gyroscopic forces to build to the extent that recovery becomes more and more difficult, or at least is delayed. Individual aircraft may have slight differences in rigging and CG. In some cases, additional recovery measures, such as full forward stick or throttle application to increase rudder and elevator power are necessary. Small aerodynamic effects, such as a slight amount of aileron deflection, can make the difference between normal recovery or not.

Why bother to conduct prolonged spins when the manoeuvre is of little value anyway, and you have to spend most of the sortie climbing to regain the altitude you have lost?

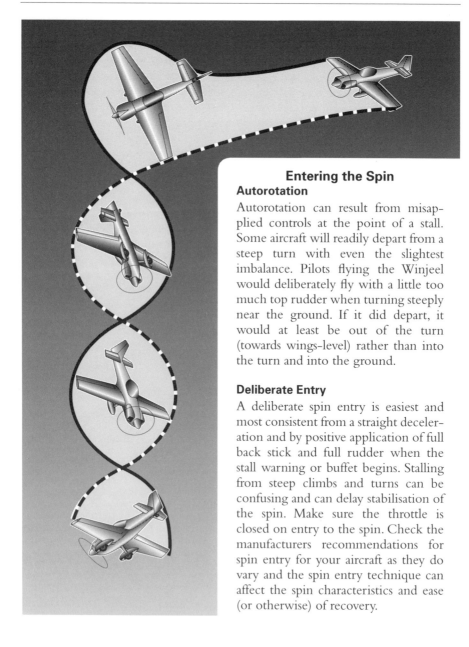

Entering the Spin
Autorotation

Autorotation can result from misapplied controls at the point of a stall. Some aircraft will readily depart from a steep turn with even the slightest imbalance. Pilots flying the Winjeel would deliberately fly with a little too much top rudder when turning steeply near the ground. If it did depart, it would at least be out of the turn (towards wings–level) rather than into the turn and into the ground.

Deliberate Entry

A deliberate spin entry is easiest and most consistent from a straight deceleration and by positive application of full back stick and full rudder when the stall warning or buffet begins. Stalling from steep climbs and turns can be confusing and can delay stabilisation of the spin. Make sure the throttle is closed on entry to the spin. Check the manufacturers recommendations for spin entry for your aircraft as they do vary and the spin entry technique can affect the spin characteristics and ease (or otherwise) of recovery.

Unintentional Departures

If the aircraft departs from controlled flight, it will not spin if the controls are immediately centralised (especially release back pressure) and the throttle is closed.

This is when we are most likely to be caught out – from a stall turn, roll-off-the-top or when pulling around the corner. The aircraft's natural stability will recover it – if you let it. Even letting go of the controls will probably avoid a spin.

Spin Recovery

There is much discussion about a universal spin recovery technique.

Use the one recommended for your aircraft by the manufacturer.

They do vary because the tailplane/rudder geometry and the rudder versus elevator power varies. Some aircraft will recover instantly the controls are released. Some require almost full forward stick. It is important to follow the sequence for your aircraft as to whether rudder or elevator is moved first.

Consider inadvertent entry from a stall with power applied or flaps extended. They will probably delay recovery so it is best to retard the throttle and retract the flaps (and undercarriage) as soon as you can.

Once you become familiar with your aircraft you will be able to time the recovery inputs so that the aircraft stabilises in a particular direction and you can use the spin as part of the aerobatic sequence – but generally a two-turn spin is sufficient for this purpose.

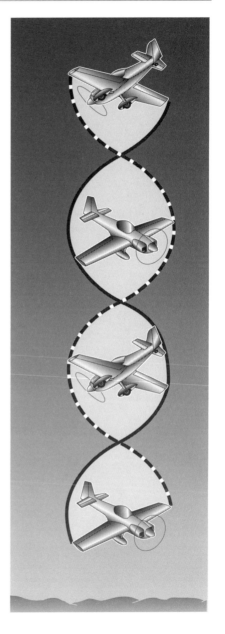

The standard recovery from any uncommanded situation or departure (i.e. other than a deliberately held spin) is:

- immediately centralise the controls; and
- close the throttle.

If the aircraft continues to rotate, apply full opposite rudder to the direction of yaw, followed by forward pressure on the control column – until full forward, if necessary. Hold these positions until the rotation stops.

For a deliberately entered spin, strictly follow the spin recovery technique advised by the aircraft manufacturer. It is important that if they say, *'full forward stick'* or *'briskly move the control column forward'*, or *'apply full opposite rudder, pause, then move the control column forwards'*, then that is exactly what you do.

What to do if the recovery doesn't seem to be working? If there is no change in the spin after two turns, confirm the direction of yaw, check the throttle is closed and reapply full rudder opposite the yaw. Then release the stick altogether and consider applying power.

Use of Power

Generally the throttle should be closed until the wings are un-stalled and the aircraft is accelerating. The gyroscopic moments from the engine and propeller can delay spin recovery or may assist. The slipstream can also be a help – but only use these options if the normal spin recovery is not satisfactory.

Non-Standard Recovery

If the aircraft does not respond, aileron towards the direction of spin will assist recovery. There is also a school of thought which suggests that letting go of the stick is the best recovery technique (with full opposite rudder applied), as a counter to possibly incorrect control inputs (certain aircraft types only). The International Aerobatic Club (which has a web site at *http://acro.harvard.edu*) has much information on, and engages in debate about, spinning.

Control Position (Especially If the Aircraft Has a Yoke)

Spinning is a balance of forces and moments. In some aircraft even a very slight amount of out-spin aileron (opposite to the direction of yaw – yet it is pro-spin) will flatten the attitude in the spin, accelerate the rate of rotation, and delay recovery. It is vital to have the ailerons neutral during the spin unless your aircraft type requires out-spin aileron to maintain a stable spin (as did the *Winjeel*). Some aircraft, also, will not remain in a spin unless the stick is held hard back, and a relaxation will allow the aircraft to accelerate into a spiral dive.

Direction of Spin

When recovering from a sustained spin it is vital to confirm the direction of spin (the direction of yaw) which in some aircraft can be confused with the direction of roll.

The turn needle of the traditional turn-and-balance indicator (the *bat* of the *bat-and-ball*) will always indicate the direction of yaw in any spin, stable or unstable, erect or inverted. When an aircraft is being tested, an extra panel of instruments is added above the coaming in the pilot's immediate field-of-view. This always includes a turn-and-balance indicator and an additional altimeter.

The turn coordinator (a similar instrument but with an aircraft symbol instead of a turn needle) has a tilted gyro which indicates both yaw and roll and so can give unreliable readings in a spin where yaw and roll can be opposite (similarly in a limited-panel, unusual attitude recovery).

Also, the skid ball does not indicate the direction of spin and can be displaced in the opposite direction during the incipient stage. The indications can even differ between the left and right side of the cockpit.

Where to Look During a Spin

It is not possible to track a single point on the horizon and watch it come around. Nor is it wise to watch the wingtip. Look ahead to watch the rotation but try to include the upper horizon in your view without trying to follow one point. If you can arrange a very prominent feature such as a runway or lake that can be watched momentarily each time it comes around then it will help keep track of the direction and number of turns.

While spinning is required to be learnt, it is better to frequently practise recovery from the incipient stage and to use the spin as if it was simply another flick roll. Incipient recovery should become second nature.

Spiral Dive

Firstly, let's state that the spiral dive is a non-event – if you have a clear horizon. The three common circumstances where the situation can be serious are as follows:
1. The aircraft is trimmed for low airspeed, say in a climb at high power, and the aircraft enters cloud. The untrained pilot allows the heading to deviate and the wings to be slightly banked – only a few degrees. The aircraft enters an almost undetectable turn. As it turns, the outer wing causes the bank to slowly and subtly increase. The nose lowers slightly and the airspeed increases a little. The longitudinal stability (because it is trimmed for a lower airspeed) causes the turn to tighten a little. The rates of roll are below the threshold of the pilot's balance mechanism in the inner ear and so no significant rolling motion is detected.

   The turn causes the wing to lift a little more. The trim tightens the turn a little and the nose lowers a little more. The airspeed increases further and the g starts to increase. The airflow noise is also building and the airspeed is now increasing noticeably, especially in a fast single with a retractable undercarriage. Now the pilot starts to feel alarmed, by the noise and building g.

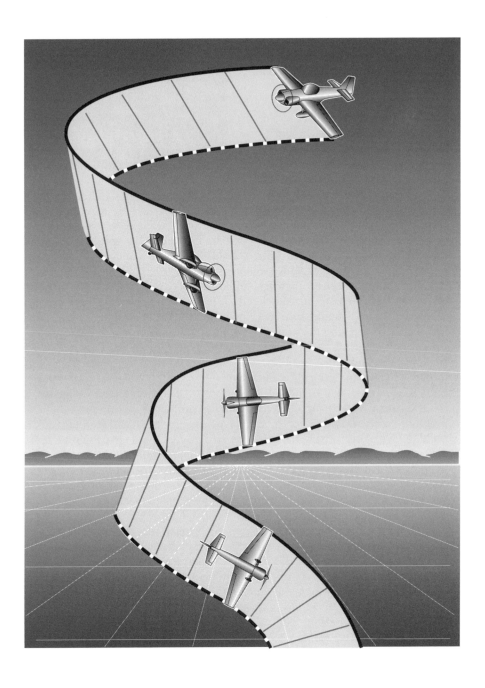

The bank increases, the turn tightens, the *g* builds, the noise builds. The outcome has two possibilities:

- the pilot sees the ground as the aircraft comes out of the bottom of the cloud and his knee-jerk reaction is to pull out, hard. This overloads the tailplane, which fails, and in the subsequent nose-down pitch, the wings fail upwards. This is the graveyard spiral which, unrecovered, leads to the loss of the aircraft, or

- the pilot levels the wings to horizontal, closes the throttle and gently raises the nose to the level attitude – a non-event if there is a clear horizon. Note that if the spiral is detected early and the throttle is closed, the pilot only has to level the wings. The nose will come up by itself as the wings are rolled to level. Indeed, the pilot may have to hold forward pressure (terrain clearance permitting) to avoid excessive rolling *g*.

2. Another common scenario is where a pilot is manoeuvring in a steep turn and allows the bank angle to increase slightly. If the pilot then increases back pressure to maintain altitude (rather than reducing bank first), the control force tightens the turn rather than raising the nose, and the load factor may become excessive. The nose will drop further and the bank will increase even more. The only recovery is to reduce the bank angle. Again, it is a non-event if there is a clear horizon.

3. The third scenario is during spinning or spin recovery. Some aircraft will not remain in a stable spin unless out-spin aileron is firmly applied throughout. If not the aircraft will slowly accelerate until it is no longer spinning and the nose will drop to a rolling dive rather than a true spin. Airspeed and load factor may build quickly. Alternatively, the spin may change to a spiral when spin recovery controls are applied and held – especially if aileron input is also applied. The aircraft may have recovered from stalled flight but the opposite rudder, forward stick and some aileron will cause it to continue to roll, yaw, pitch forward and now accelerate. The increase in airspeed will result in an increase in *g* and in roll and yaw rate. The pilot can now be disorientated, especially if he is just recovering from a prolonged spin in the opposite direction and the whole balance mechanism has neutralised to that motion. The tendency is to maintain the control input or to centralise. At this stage, the aircraft has a pronounced nose-down attitude, is accelerating, and rolling rapidly. The trim will be tightening the turn. Altitude and time is running out. At least the throttle was left closed – or was it?

In any of these cases, the recovery is very easy, especially if it is initiated early and provided that there is a clearly defined horizon. In small business they say that the three vital requirements for success are *'location, location, location'* – provided you start with *'capital, capital, capital'*. For aerobatic flight, the three requirements are *'horizon, horizon, horizon'* – provided you start with *'altitude, altitude, altitude'*.

Escape Routes

The Nearest Horizon

You will hear frequent reference to the *nearest horizon*. What is it? Simply the horizon which it would take the least pitch to reach. Initially it is easier to explain if we look at an external view of the aircraft; then we'll see the corresponding pilot's field-of-view. In this instance, peripheral view is very important. Let's see what we can see.

Clearly inverted:

Erect but steeply nose-down:

The most difficult decision – inverted and nose-down. Roll then pull.

The visual pattern can be subtle, in which case you are almost vertical.

As a general rule, it is better to roll the aircraft until a horizon comes into view
– and then recover from the dive.

Mishandled or Misjudged Manoeuvres

High roll-rate may not seem like a luxury for the more capable aerobatic aircraft, and this is certainly true. Unfortunately, it is not appreciated how important it can be for pilot survival in any aircraft. The design standards for training aircraft do not place any emphasis on this feature. If ever you get into trouble, safety lies in the ability to quickly regain straight-and-level controlled flight with minimum loss of altitude. This is usually achieved by rolling and then pulling. If the aircraft is sluggish in roll, the aircraft is accelerating and losing altitude and there is little the pilot can do about it. Some pro-verse rudder may help a little but not much as it cannot generate anything like the rolling power that the ailerons can provide – and you risk a departure.

The answer is not to commit the nose too low if you have any doubt about the clearance. This is especially true of the second half of the barrel roll – as we will discuss later. If in doubt, roll out. Better still, never get into this situation. Some aircraft have a very sluggish rate-of-roll.

Nose-Low Recoveries

A nose-low recovery to controlled flight is simply a sequence which contains the airspeed and allows a gentle recovery to straight-and-level flight without over-stressing the aircraft. It is exactly the same as the spiral dive recovery.

Nose-High Recoveries

A nose-high recovery seeks to avoid a stall and departure from controlled flight. Like any other departure, the immediate actions are to centralise the control column and rudder. Then it remains to simply hold everything (firmly) and then wait until the nose is below the horizon and the aircraft is accelerating. Control the RPM with the throttle.

If the nose-high attitude is not extreme, pushing forwards to a level attitude and simultaneously applying full power may recover the situation. However, this is not a comfortable recovery, and if left too late there is a risk of departure with full power applied.

Extreme Attitude and Vertical Recoveries

The importance of containing airspeed

When fully vertical or close to it, there are two short-term concerns and two longer-term:

Short-term:
- Avoid any departure by centralising the controls and closing the throttle.
- Avoid damage to the controls by firmly holding the stick and rudder pedals.
- Then wait for the longer-term.

Longer-term:
- Avoid overspeed of the engine by controlling the throttle application.
- Avoid over-stressing the airframe by gently applying *g* as soon as the aircraft is flying and you have a decent horizontal reference, but back-off as the aircraft accelerates.

Vertical Recoveries

As soon as there is reversed airflow, caused by backwards or tumbling flight, there is risk of airframe damage to the control surfaces, trim tabs, hinges and control linkages.

Vertical recoveries are taught as part of your training because they may be necessary in the event of being hung-up during an attempted stall turn or other vertical manoeuvre – even a mishandled loop.

A semi-vertical climb will end in a sudden nose-up (nose-back) or nose-down (nose-forward) pitch (hammer-head) through the vertically down attitude and via a slight oscillation, a vertical dive. This, in itself, is tolerable if the control surfaces are not allowed to move.

Propeller RPM must be contained in the dive by retarding the throttle or applying g as soon as the aircraft accelerates through V_S.

If the climb was truly vertical, the aircraft will slide rearwards until the reversed airflow builds in intensity and any slight imbalance in pitching moments causes a violent pitch over through the vertical. If there is a finite delay and the airspeed has built to any degree, the reversed airflow can be of such intensity that it can snatch the control column out of the pilot's grasp and bang the control surfaces to full deflection. In specially designed aircraft there are control stops to absorb this violence. In most aircraft there are none and permanent damage can result.

Torque effects and the gyroscopic loads on the engine mounts can be considerable.

It is always better to upset a dead vertical position with rudder, then centralise and hang on.

Tailslides

If the vertical climb is allowed to continue to its logical conclusion, there will be a momentary tailslide, and then a violent pitch. Depending on the exact flightpath, the aircraft may pitch forwards or backwards (backwards is more comfortable).

The subsequent flightpath and recovery action is similar.

For most situations, it is better to apply and hold rudder deflection to avoid reverse airflow and reverse airspeed building up. If a stall turn goes awry, centralise the control column, close the throttle and hang on – but keep the rudder applied until the aircraft starts to yaw. It is insurance against the reverse flow.

If the aircraft departs into an incipient spin, then centralise everything.

It is sometimes recommended that the throttle be closed when a vertical recovery is imminent. However, leaving power applied provides the greatest elevator and rudder power and therefore the greatest control. Also, the violence of the pitch is dampened (cushioned) by the airflow.

The RPM has to be contained when the aircraft is accelerating downwards.

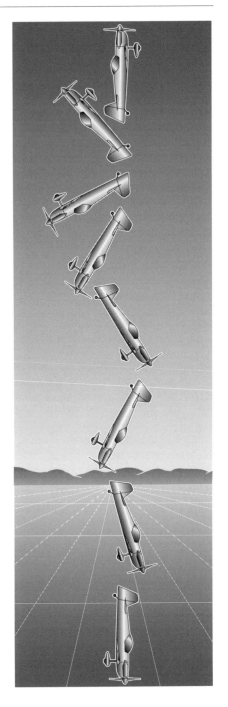

The Winjeel was an Australian military training aircraft used in the sixties and seventies. (Winjeel is an aboriginal word meaning little eagle). It was powered by a 450 hp Pratt and Whitney radial and was a pleasant aerobatic aircraft although it would readily depart from controlled flight if mishandled. It was not unlike the piston Provost in form and size. It had conventional controls and, because of the massive engine, had rudder trim as well as elevator trim.

On Friday afternoons there was no cadet training and the instructors were allocated time to refine their own flying and instructional skills. On one such mutual sortie the instructors were exploring the boundaries of flying skill and decided (before the concept of Cockpit or Crew Resource Management – CRM) if they could work as a crew and fly the aircraft on trim alone – with one instructor handling the elevator trim, and the other the throttle and rudder trim. This proved too easy as they entered turns, climbs and glides.

So they decided a stall turn would be a more appropriate challenge. The dive and entry was straightforward, and as the aircraft reached the vertical position, one instructor was rapidly winding the elevator trim forward from the 3g pull-up to maintain the vertical 0g climb, and at the appropriate moment the other wound in full rudder trim. The trim proved insufficient to yaw the aircraft and it started a tail slide. Before the instructors could react, the elevators were violently forced beyond full deflection and the control linkage was broken.

The aircraft completed a natural but violent hammerhead and the instructors were able to recover from the ensuing dive with the elevator trim (the rudder trim having been reset). They successfully returned for a safe landing using the same technique.

So that's the theory of manoeuvring flight. Soon we'll see it put into practice – but first let's look at the effect on the human body and the preparation necessary to carry us safely through aerobatic manoeuvres.

Chapter 3

The Physiology of Manoeuvring Flight

The human is not designed for the airborne environment. We can, however, be trained and we can, to some extent, become acclimatised.

We know the limitations that we suffer as a result of our being designed and evolved to stand vertically erect on the earth, to move slowly and to feel the force of gravity. In flight, the body is subjected to forces and motions which are complex and which can cause the senses to become confused. In most cases, this is not a problem, provided there's a clear visual horizon. With our dominant visual sense, all other inputs are easily overridden and we can virtually ignore other cues.

The process of learning aerobatics, in terms of physiological aspects, is one of acclimatising the body to the motions, the rates of yaw, pitch and roll, to load-factors or *g*, and to the confusing sensations caused by simultaneous motions and accelerations in different planes.

In learning aerobatics, we actually go through a process, as in learning anything in life, of acquiring a skill and de-sensitising those senses which are redundant or not able to accommodate the new motion.

Aerobatic training is also about building an awareness of what to look for, what to expect, what to do about it, and what to do if it goes wrong.

What we call *g,* or load-factor, is the total acceleration that both the structure of the aircraft and the body of the pilot feel during manoeuvring flight. It is a combination of a normal force of gravity plus the accelerated loads caused by the changing flightpath. Total load factor is the force of gravity plus or minus the applied (additional) load factor.

How Does an Aircraft Manoeuvre?

You will recall from Newton's Laws of Motion, that a body wishes to continue in a state of rest or uniform motion in a straight line, unless acted upon by an external force. In the case of our aircraft, the fuselage and its contents, including the pilot, wish to continue in a straight line at uniform speed. As you know, in normal flight, lift equals weight, and even in shallow climb or descent, there's not much difference. If the wings generate two or three times the lift in comparison to the weight, that excess force causes the aircraft to accelerate in the direction of that force.

When an aircraft manoeuvres, what happens? The pilot increases the angle of attack of the wing and the increased angle of attack generates an excess of lift. This excess of lift then changes the flightpath of the aircraft.

The load is transferred from the wing to the fuselage through the wing-root and struts.

Thus the wings accelerate the fuselage in the direction of the excess lift. The fuselage, through the floor of the cockpit, pushes the pilot's seat upwards, the pilot's seat compresses the body from the bottom to the head. (What the pilot feels effectively is that he/she is being squashed down into the seat). In fact, what is happening is that the pilot's seat is squashing his/her spine up towards the head.

When we stand upon the earth, we experience one force of gravity (g). This force of gravity is proportional to the mass of the object and produces the same acceleration for all falling bodies. Therefore as a measure of load factor (force or acceleration), we can use this universal unit of g for any object of any size. In aviation, acceleration is expressed in multiples of the acceleration due to gravity, g (9.81 metres per second per second, mps^2 or 32.2 fps^2). If the wings generate twice as much lift (force) as required to balance the weight, then that will accelerate the aircraft in that direction at twice the acceleration due to gravity. The force experienced by the structure and by the pilot is twice the force of gravity, or $2g$. If the wing generates three times the lift, then the force felt by the fuselage and the pilot is $3g$, and so on.

Literally the seat pushes upwards at two or three times the compression due to normal gravity and we feel the compression of supporting a head and shoulders two or three times its normal weight. It is as if you were now carrying two or three heads. As well as the effect on the body's structure or skeleton, it affects everything within the body that has substance or mass. Everything experiences this force.

Physiological Symptoms of Load Factor

We are not designed to be manoeuvred. Thus to tolerate forces higher than $+1g$ we have to compensate. The body at $+1g$ can easily function. The heart can pump blood around the total circulatory system, whether it be down to the toes, to the tip of the fingers or up to the head. At $+2g$, literally everything in the pilot's body weighs twice as much as normal, including the blood. As well as overcoming the friction of pumping the blood through what may be partly constricted arteries (or older arteries – take note), the heart has to manoeuvre blood weighing twice as much to the extremities of the head and the toes. In a standing or sitting position, there's no difficulty getting the blood flow to the feet. However, there is some difficulty getting it back from the feet to the heart. Similarly, the heart has difficulty maintaining blood flow to the head. At $+3g$, the heart has to work three times as hard. At $+4g$, four times. Eventually the eyes and the brain suffer from this reduced blood supply. Vision becomes narrowed, colour perception disappears and eventually all vision is lost. There can follow total loss of consciousness.

We can develop our capacity to tolerate g. The body is very adaptable, and like most things, it acquires a resistance and an ability to function in unusual situations. The first effect of a reduction of blood supply to the head is on vision and on the brain function. With experience, though, a pilot can readily tolerate $4g$ for short periods.

There are physical techniques that you can use, such as tensing the stomach and leg muscles, to help prevent the blood pooling in the lower limbs.

Grey-Out, Black-Out and *g*-loc

Speed has relatively little effect on the human body, whereas acceleration or deceleration may produce pronounced effects ranging from fatigue to a complete collapse of the cardiovascular system.

The brain and eyes need a continuous supply of oxygen. They have little storage capacity, so strong or prolonged g forces, which reduce the supply, lead progressively to reduced visual acuity, loss of colour vision, loss of sight and even unconsciousness. When the acceleration is centripetal, as in turn or pitching manoeuvre, it is felt by the pilot as an increase in weight. In a 60° banked level turn, you will experience $2g$, or feel twice as heavy.

As soon as the blood flow to the brain or to the eyes is reduced, then there are physical symptoms. There is some sensation of dizziness or tingling of the brain, the vision becomes focused ahead and we start to lose the peripheral vision. This condition is called *tunnel vision*. Continuing the g we start to lose colour vision. This is called *grey-out*.

Further increasing g forces will lead to total loss of vision, or *black-out*. At this point, the pilot is temporarily blind, though still conscious. Further g increase will inevitably lead to insufficient oxygen and sugar supply to keep the brain functioning and so to g-induced loss of consciousness (*g-loc*).

A sequence of sight-related changes occurs before unconsciousness. As these visual symptoms occur while the pilot is conscious, they can be controlled and relieved. Relaxing the back pressure on the controls will bring nearly-instantaneous relief from the degraded sight condition. The grey-out to black-out phenomena occur so as to act as a warning, a *threshold of potential unconsciousness*. They are the signal to reduce the control pressure. These symptoms occur at the normal rate-of-*g* onset. However, in this case, there is appreciable lag or delay before the effects are felt, and there is time to return to normal.

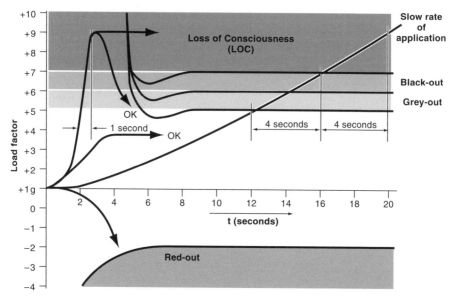

If, however, the rate of application of *g* is rapid, the warning signals, of degraded sight, are bypassed. If the *g* is then sustained, the pilot will become instantly unconscious. If you do black out you will, intuitively, relax the control pressure to reduce the *g*, immediately regain full sight, and remain conscious throughout. However, if you lose consciousness, it takes at least 15 seconds to recover and during this time you can be very disoriented. Loss of consciousness is a debilitating experience. If you have seen someone faint, you will recall how disoriented and incapable they were during the recovery period.

A-loc

Another term that has been recently coined is *a-loc*. A-loc is *almost* loss of consciousness due to *g*. The reason for the differentiation is that, even if the pilot does not lose consciousness, there is a temporary period of confusion and even euphoria, where the pilot either does not recognise, or does not care about, the seriousness of the situation. It is momentary but has caused some unexplained pilot lack-of-response during recovery from high-*g* manoeuvres.

Recovery

In all cases, if the load factor is removed as soon as the first symptoms appear, the body very quickly recovers to normal. It is only in extremely violent situations, in which the rate of onset of *g* is very high and the *g* is then sustained, that the pilot can momentarily lose consciousness. Even when the *g* factor is removed, there can be a period of confusion. This is believed to have caused several flying display accidents to combat aircraft. For us, *g* is not a problem. We will build up the aerobatic routine and repertoire of manoeuvres slowly and in logical sequence so that initially we only have the mild *g* manoeuvres and we will be subjected only to positive *g*. That is, the force retains us in the seat rather than tries to push us out of the seat.

With *g* application, we will also acclimatise the body to high rates of onset and high rates of manoeuvre. These do compound the problem, but once again, provided there is a clearly defined horizon and we anticipate the manoeuvre, the body has no particular difficulty in orienting itself and coping with mild levels of *g*.

Pilot Protection

At load factors much beyond +4*g*, we have to provide assistance to the pilot. You may have heard of *g suits* (or, more correctly, *anti-g suits*) that are worn by fighter pilots. The suit consists of a pair of inflatable trousers, which compress the legs and lower abdomen, thus forcing the blood to remain in the upper body and reducing the pooling in the lower limbs. This considerably assists the heart in maintaining sufficient oxygenated blood to the eyes and brain. We can also increase tolerance by reducing the vertical distance between legs, head and heart.

The famous Focke-Wulf 190 had a second set of rudder pedals above the first, so that for combat (when the brakes were not required!), the pilot legs would be raised to the higher position and thereby reduce the vertical distance from the heart. This reduced pooling of the blood. Many competition aerobatic aircraft also have elevated rudder pedals.

The F16 and competition aerobatic aircraft also have a semi-reclined seating position for the pilot to reduce the vertical displacement of blood from the heart. Inclination is limited by the need to be able to eject and the need to see.

In the fifties, aircraft were trialled with the pilot in a prone position (e.g. the prone Meteor). But this caused other problems, such as the need to support the chin, difficulty in looking over the shoulder, and difficulty operating the controls.

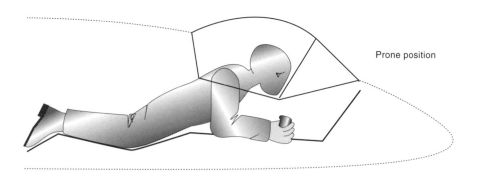

The other factor that affects the body's disability is the duration of the applied load. Most sustained aerobatic manoeuvres, such as the loop, take 30 seconds or less and only require $+4g$. Therefore the amount and the duration of g can be managed. Very-high-g manoeuvres are violent by nature and by necessity of short duration. If we plan an aerobatic sequence so that we have gentle manoeuvres in between the high-g manoeuvres, then the body can rest and relax and be prepared for the sustained g or for the sudden peak-g applications.

This is one of the reasons why it is much more difficult to fly as a passenger in aerobatic flight than as the pilot. The pilot knows what's coming next, and so by controlling the rate of application and the duration, the pilot can relax the *g* when he/she feels symptoms of load factor.

Negative *g*

Negative *g* is the acceleration experienced when the pilot's head is outside the manoeuvre and thus the blood (and everything else) is forced away from the floor of the cockpit. It is most uncomfortable as the body is supported entirely by the harness, and any loose object, including dirt, dust, pencils, coins and mud, will float or hit the canopy (unless you have an open cockpit).

Negative *g* manoeuvres are really beyond the scope of this book for other than inverted flight ($-1g$). Aside from the discomfort and the feeling of insecurity, one does adapt to quite high levels of negative *g,* but these are expert manoeuvres in special aircraft. Going directly from negative to positive *g* also induces *a-loc.*

Symptoms of excessive negative *g* include blood-shot eyes, headaches and even burst blood vessels. Pilots also talk of a condition known as **red-out** where the field-of-view becomes discoloured because the lower eyelid moves over the eye, and there is also excess blood in the eyeball. With negative *g* there is no *g*-suit protection, although semi-reclined seating still helps.

How the Body Senses Motion and Which Way Is Up

Hearing and Balance

Although sight is the most important sense for flying, visual messages to the brain are reinforced or, at times, contradicted by messages from other sensory organs, especially the balance mechanisms in the inner ear (*vestibular* inputs), as well as skin and muscular feeling from all over the body (*seat-of-the-pants* or tactile inputs, known as *somatosensory* inputs).

The ear provides two senses – hearing and balance:
- *hearing* allows us to perceive sounds and to interpret them; and
- *balance* lets us know which way is up and whether or not we are accelerating.

Sound is energy that we can detect with our ears. It can be useful and pleasant, as with voice messages and music, but excessive sound is fatiguing, and can even lead to damage within the ear. Sound waves may be felt through the bone structure.

Sound signals are caused by pressure waves travelling through the air, and these cause sensitive membranes of the eardrum to oscillate. The inner ear translates these pressure vibrations into electrical signals which are sent via the auditory nerve to the brain, where they are interpreted. Sound cues are important to the aerobatic pilot for airspeed and propeller RPM.

Balance and acceleration signals, from the inner ear, pass to the brain as electrical signals for interpretation, but the sensors are designed for a different environment.

The Structure of the Ear

The ear is divided into three areas: the outer, middle, and inner ear.

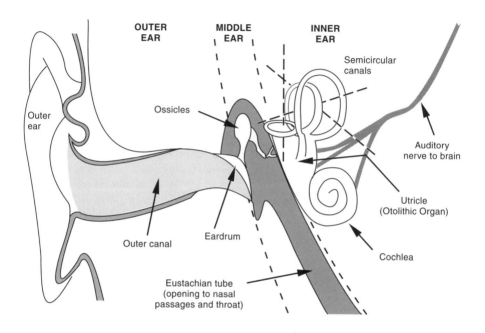

The outer ear includes:
- the external ear (known medically as the *pinna* or *auricle*), which is used to gather the sound signals;
- the outer canal through which the pressure waves pass; and
- the eardrum, which is caused to vibrate in harmony with the pressure waves.

Any obstruction to the outer canal, such as earplugs or an excess of wax, can reduce the sound pressure waves reaching the eardrum. Similarly, a padded cover over the external ear will reduce the sound waves entering the ear.

The middle ear is an air-filled cavity containing three small bones, known as *ossicles*, which are moved by the vibrating eardrum, converting the pressure wave energy into mechanical energy of motion. The ossicles are arranged like a series of levers to increase the effect of the initial movement. This movement then passes on to the cochlea in the inner ear.

The air in the middle ear is maintained at ambient pressure via the *Eustachian tube,* which connects the interior of the middle ear to the nasal passages. There is (or should be) no leakage of air across the eardrum, and there should be easy passage of air through the Eustachian tube to equalise pressures – for instance, when climbing or descending. (This is sometimes hindered by swelling and inflammation when a person has a cold, and can lead to serious consequences if a person flies with a cold or similar infection.)

Interference to the movement of the three small ossicles or their joints will reduce or distort the sound signal. This can be caused by ear infections, damage to the bones or joints, or a blocked ear with air trapped inside the middle ear (*barotitis*).

The inner ear contains two very important elements:

- The *cochlea* for hearing; it converts the mechanical energy from the ossicles into electrical signals which then travel via the auditory nerve to the brain for interpretation. Excessive noise can lead to damage of the hairs in the cochlea, and infection or injury can damage the auditory nerve, possibly causing ringing in the ears (tinnitus).
- The *vestibular apparatus* consists of three fluid-filled semicircular canals. Each has a cluster of small hairs at their base. Interaction between the fluid in the canals and the hairs provides sensations of movement – in the three axes of flight – and resulting electrical signals sent to the brain as orientation information. The sensing hairs sit at the base of each semicircular canal in a chamber known as the 'cupula'. In the same region is the *otolithic* organ (also called the *utricle*), a device which detects linear acceleration or deceleration. It is co-located with, but separate from, the vestibular apparatus.

The ear is never switched off, and loud or particular noises to which we have a conditioned response can always help stir us from even the deepest sleep. It is interesting to note how you can extract messages important for you out of a noisy background – for instance, a radio message directed at you, the sound of your own child on a crowded beach, or your own name mentioned in a distant conversation – known as 'the cocktail party effect'.

Manoeuvre Rates

If you rotate a full cup of tea, you will see that initially the cup will rotate but the fluid hesitates, until the friction with the walls of the cup causes it to start to move. Eventually, this friction between the tea molecules will cause the whole contents of the cup to rotate at a uniform speed. If we then stop the cup the fluid will initially continue at its original speed until friction causes it to slow. A thicker (more viscous), stickier fluid will not hesitate as much. This lag is the means by which the sensors of the inner ear (the semicircular canals) detect radial (rotational) motion and acceleration.

The semicircular canals work in exactly the same way as the cup of tea.

Tilting or rolling
(lagging fluid
tilts hair)

Balanced turn or
steady (slow) roll rate
(hairs erect)

We have three canals – one in each axis so that pitch, roll and yaw are each sensed as a change in relative speed or rest, between the canal and its fluid contents. The change will remain until the body's rotation ceases or becomes steady (i.e. there is no longer any acceleration).

There are also two linear channels – one horizontal and one vertical. These *otoliths* sense linear speed changes fore-and-aft, as on a motor-cycle, and up-and-down, as in a lift, respectively.

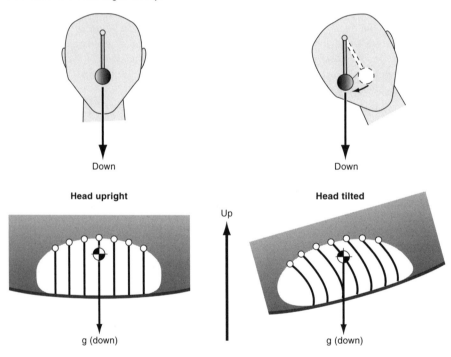

Down

Down

Head upright

Head tilted

Up

g (down)

g (down)

While we have a clearly defined horizon there is an overpowering order in what we sense. The visual channel keeps us oriented. All other cues either endorse what we see (and are therefore accepted) or they conflict (and are overruled).

In the absence of a horizon we rely on the force of gravity as our sense of verticality – modified by any rotational or linear acceleration sensed by the inner ear or the body in general (e.g. being pressed into the seat or against the side of the cockpit).

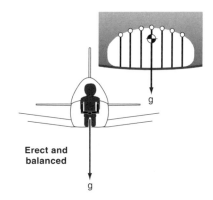

Erect and balanced

g

g

If we add centrifugal reaction caused by manoeuvring, as well as the pitch, roll and yaw rates, then the senses have trouble coping.

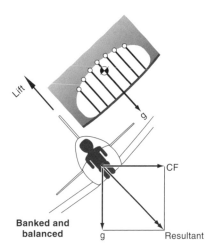

Lift

g

CF

Banked and balanced

g

Resultant

Disorientation

Further, beyond four or five continuous rotations the fluids in the inner ear catch up and the sense of acceleration is removed. They now sense no motion. Thus in a sustained spin or a series of consecutive rapid rolls, they are now stable and a spin recovery can actually be wrongly sensed as a spin entry in the opposite direction. The sensation can be sufficiently powerful to cause the pilot to reduce or remove spin recovery controls with potentially fatal consequences.

Consecutive, rapid rolls or prolonged spins cause misalignment of the body's senses. It is wise not to enter a high *g* manoeuvre immediately following rapid rotations. Pause in straight-and-level flight for a few seconds to allow the semicircular fluids to catch up. In the Mirage, which would roll at nearly twice a second, it was usual to follow a series of consecutive rolls with a roll in the opposite direction to realign the pilot's personal *gyros*.

Rate of roll does not cause as much distress to the body – within the capabilities of normal aerobatic training aircraft - unless the rolling is continued through four or five uninterrupted rolls. Competition aircraft, such as the CAP 232 and Sukhoi 31, are capable of very high rates of roll (in excess of 400 degrees-per-second) which if sustained, can actually lead to disorientation. The tendency is particularly powerful if the horizon is less than clearly defined. The other occasion where we will experience high manoeuvre rates is in the developed spin. The aircraft is rolling, pitching and yawing and, in some cases, there could be an additional oscillatory motion or rocking. The combination of rapid and changing roll and yaw, especially if the pilot looks ahead at the ground rather than the horizon, can be quite alarming. It is yet another experience for the pilot to accommodate.

If you watch a professional dancer or skater you will notice that, as they spin on the tip of their toes, they watch one point and track it for part of the turn and then quickly pivot their head to regain the same point and once again track it. This prevents dizziness and disorientation. However, this reference is not generally available to the pilot. If you have ever spun around with your head aligned to your body and then suddenly stop. Not unexpectedly, you would probably fall over.

With high rates of rotation, we are vulnerable to similar disorientation while spinning or rolling. After several turns, the balance mechanism no longer senses the rotation. The eyes have only a blurred view of the earth. When the spin stops, the body is alarmed to sense that it is rotating in the opposite direction (even though it isn't – the stopping is sensed as acceleration in the opposite direction).

The Body's Ability to Cope with *g* and Manoeuvre Rates

Fitness and Recency

A normal, medically fit and physically fit human can readily adapt to the loads and manoeuvre rates of a normal aerobatic training aircraft. However, if you take an older body, a less fit body, a body lacking sleep, a body suffering the effect of a hangover or a body that smokes, the tolerance levels are adversely affected. Tests conducted by the United States Air Force suggest that a moderate, balanced programme of aerobics and weight training is best. Extreme aerobic training can actually reduce your tolerance to *g* because of the increased capacity of the blood vessels and lower pulse-rate under stress.

Recent practice affects the pilot's ability to cope. Competition and display pilots go through a comprehensive and sustained build-up of both their physical fitness and their aerobatic training to reach the peak values that they can tolerate.

To learn aerobatics, and to continue developing, requires the pilot to fly relatively frequently. A gap of even two or three weeks between sorties will show a noticeable reduction in the pilot's capacity to cope with g and manoeuvres rates. It is essential (and common sense) that if you haven't flown for a while, some preliminary time should be spent working-up to the peak g levels and manoeuvre rates.

An aerobatic training programme should cater for this, and there should also always be a refresher period before embarking on display sequences. If you haven't had the opportunity to fly for several weeks, or maybe even months, then either take the time to slowly work back to the routine, or even carry out a dual sortie with an instructor until you are again up to speed.

Rate of Application/Onset of *g*

Another consideration with manoeuvring is the change of g level. The aircraft structure flexes with the applied load. Flexing is greatest when going from one extreme to the other, so bending of the structure is greatest when going from high negative g values to high positive g and vice versa. Similarly, the body is more stressed by such extremes, e.g. from $-1g$ inverted flight to a $+5g$ pull-up, and this is when the g-loc phenomenon has most frequently been observed. While it may be less spectacular, it is safer for the aircraft and the pilot to relax the positive or negative g, pause in unaccelerated flight and then apply the next loading. The most dangerous transition is probably from high values of negative g directly to high positive g. A simple solution is to pause in erect $+1g$ flight for a moment to settle down. It is easy to build this into a programme.

It is actually possible for the aircraft to be damaged – without the pilot feeling the full amount of g. A sudden application (called a *snatch-pull*) which is applied then immediately removed is felt in its entirety by the structure, but the body still is settling and accommodating the full load. An instant pull has been known to cause permanent damage to the structure and even in-flight break-up of the aircraft.

Airsickness

Anyone learning aerobatics and spinning may feel uneasy or queasy until the body acclimatises and gets to know the sensations associated with the different manoeuvres. Some aircraft smell of fuel during manoeuvres and this aggravates any feeling of sickness. Make sure there is plenty of fresh air and pause between manoeuvres. Keep the horizon in sight at all times. Fly regularly.

You may feel uneasy when the instructor is flying, but most discomfort disappears when you are flying yourself. Most of all, approach the training with a positive attitude. Any ill-feeling will pass and you will come to enjoy aerobatics.

Stress and Anxiety

It is normal to feel some apprehension before aerobatic flying. This will diminish with recent and regular practice under the tutelage of a mature, responsible instructor. Stress from daily life is unavoidable, and while the advice is to leave it on the ground, it is not always possible.

In fact, one of the compelling reasons for aerobatics (or car racing, or rock climbing) is that it requires such total concentration that you are forced to forget other problems. This change of mental focus is as refreshing as sleep.

If you are still feeling anxious about aerobatic flying after several sorties then discuss it openly with your instructor. Stifling anxiety causes it to build up – like the kite rising against the wind. It may be that certain manoeuvres or feelings are of concern and they may be rectifiable or avoidable.

Aerobatics in a Hot Climate

The cockpit workload in an aerobatic aircraft is high. It is even more so when you are a beginner. Aerobatic flying in a hot climate is very demanding and it is important to take extra precautions. If it is fitted with a canopy, the aerobatic aircraft will have large areas of clear transparency to maximise field-of-view. This means that the cockpit air will heat up quickly in summer. The pilot is also exposed directly to radiant heat and sunburn. It is important to cover the neck, head and forearms. Wear a hat and sunscreen. The fabric or leather flying helmet with inbuilt headset is good.

Perspiration can be a problem too. A helmet or a headband is useful in keeping sweat out of your eyes. Wear loose-fitting clothes of natural fibre next to the skin. Wash away any fuel or oil that you may have contacted during the pre-flight, otherwise it will sting when you perspire. Gloves help to overcome the problem of sweaty hands slipping off the controls.

Most aircraft are designed for temperate climates and little attention is given to added cockpit ventilation for very hot weather. (In some aircraft it is possible to disconnect the heater and use the hot air vents for additional cool air.)

Dehydration can be a serious risk. Drink plenty of water and discontinue the sortie if there is any feeling of tiredness, confusion, dizziness or dryness. You may take a water container if it can be stowed safely.

Thermal activity adds difficulty and risk of over-stress. Also, summer haze may obscure the horizon. Fly early morning or evening, or choose a higher altitude where haze and thermals are minimised. It is also cooler up there – although manoeuvre potential is reduced at altitude.

The wearing of parachutes is mandatory in some countries – but they do add to the potential heat stress. Sheepskin seat covers are a wonderful means of reducing the build-up of perspiration on the back and seat.

Chapter 4

Control Technique and Feel

As Olivia once said, 'Feel your way.' (Saturday Night Fever)

The most important ability or sensitivity of the skilled aerobatic pilot (or any pilot for that matter) is the feel for the aircraft. Wolfgang Langeweische (*Stick and Rudder*, McGraw-Hill) expressed it beautifully when he referred to the *buoyancy* of the aircraft. This buoyancy, or latent ability to manoeuvre, is something a pilot comes to know if he/she flies one aircraft type frequently. It is the potential excess lift, the reserve capacity to instantaneously change flightpath, the stored energy, the coiled spring – all of this is *buoyancy*.

An aircraft at low airspeed is not only sluggish in response, its wing is close to the critical angle of attack. It may have plenty of excess thrust, but until it actually accelerates to a higher airspeed, it cannot apply even moderate *g*. Thus it has little ability to manoeuvre. An aircraft that is also at low altitude has no potential energy to exchange for speed and so is doubly vulnerable. You can study all about the control inputs and speed, but the essence of learning aerobatics is the development of this feel for the buoyancy of the aircraft. The essence of finesse is to:

- feel the *g*;
- feel the onset of buffet;
- feel the floating controls;
- feel the adverse yaw;
- feel the sideslip;
- feel the stick-force lightening;
- listen to the engine;
- hear the airflow and speed; and even
- listen to the silence.

While buoyancy determines our ability to change the flightpath, it is excess thrust that allow us to accelerate or to maintain speed at high climb angles or high angles of attack.

We have no direct indication of the lift potential (unless we have an angle of attack indicator which shows how much spare, or reserve, angle of attack, we have available, at any time). However, we do have a crude indication of potential excess thrust just by seeing how much MAP and/or RPM are set compared to the maximum allowable or the maximum continuous – as the case may be. However, we don't want to be looking inside. We need to develop another sensitivity – to the sound of the engine, the sound of the airflow and the position of the throttle lever relative to fully forward and to fully closed. We can develop a similar sensitivity to the position of the stick in relation to the fully forward or fully rearward position – it is the *thermometer* (yardstick) of our buoyancy.

Manoeuvring on the threshold, or edge, of the buffet onset is a valuable exercise in learning the symptoms of your aircraft at high angles of attack. From normal cruise speed at maximum continuous power, enter a steep turn and tighten until there is stall warning or preferably a hint of aerodynamic buffet. Obviously, induced drag increases at this time. Hold the back pressure to keep the buffet just noticeable and prevent any further speed decay by increasing bank and letting the nose lower. Fly on the edge of the buffet, playing bank angle against airspeed. Roll out and reverse the turn or maintain the slight buffet and reverse the turn direction if you have enough energy. It's a terrific way of developing sensitivity to the highest lift potential that your aircraft can offer.

The wonderful old Vampire had a subtle *burble* or weak buffet before the drag increased significantly. You could manoeuvre the aircraft keeping it on the burble and so achieve the absolute maximum turning performance at any speed.

Energy Management

The secret of success for aerobatic manoeuvring is managing the energy of the aircraft. If the aircraft slows, we need to apply power to offset the increase in induced drag to avoid continuing to decelerate until the point of stalling. Similarly, if we wish to apply +3 or 4g to enter a loop, we also have to balance the same increase in induced drag by an increase in thrust. As the nose drops or the g is relaxed and the aircraft accelerates, we have to reduce thrust to avoid exceeding limiting speeds or engine RPM. It is the mark of a good pilot, aerobatic or otherwise, that all the time he's making control inputs to manoeuvre the aircraft, he's making equivalent thrust changes to manage the energy through the flight profile.

Altitude is stored energy. Fighters never engage unless they have an altitude advantage or excess speed (zoom potential) – aerobatics is no different.

Taking into account the performance of the aircraft type requires sensitivity and planning. A series of continuous loops will consume energy quickly. Not using full power when the nose is above the horizon wastes potential altitude gain and therefore potential energy. Not applying full power in anticipation of high g, high alpha and high drag unnecessarily decays airspeed.

What Does All This Mean?

When planning a manoeuvre, allow for altitude to convert into entry speed. Allow the aircraft to accelerate to entry speed quickly by avoiding excessive g in the preceding turn or wing-over. Apply full power smoothly as soon as you apply g and at about the same rate. Apply g smoothly and avoid any sign of buffet – i.e. relax the g a little if you feel stick lightening or buffet. Apply aileron smoothly, but not suddenly, even when you need full deflection.

Where To Look – Leading With Your Chin

A useful practice is to always direct your attention, eyes and head in the direction that you wish to go. Staying *ahead* of the aircraft in this way prepares the whole body for the following manoeuvre. Look for the next horizon - the one in the direction you will be going - but also keep part of the aircraft structure within your peripheral view if possible.

The eyes lead and look out, the head follows, then the hands and feet move the controls. The aircraft responds and the eyes and other senses check the response of the aircraft – and make adjustments if necessary. Watch a dancer or gymnast.

When planning a sequence, plan low-g manoeuvres, such as wing-overs and stall turns, in between high-g manoeuvres and use the thrust and upward momentum in these vertical manoeuvres to maximise altitude gain and minimise altitude loss – i.e. nose up, full power – nose down, reduce power (unless applying g).

Technique

The technique for various aerobatic manoeuvres has to be modified to suit the aircraft type and its limitations – whether system or performance. It's just like the overtaking manoeuvre in a car. If you have plenty of excess power then the manoeuvre is not critical. If you are in an under-powered vehicle passing a truck on a hill then the manoeuvre requires judgement and timing to build up excess energy and pull out at the right time, and you need an escape route!

For example, basic aerobatic aircraft (called *limited aerobatic, semi-aerobatic* or *utility category,* as distinct from *fully aerobatic*) are typically limited in excess thrust and control response as well as ultimate load factor. Such aircraft are not capable of all manoeuvres and suffer reduced performance to the extent that special techniques have to be employed.

An aircraft such as a Chipmunk or Cessna Aerobat has to be climbed to a start point sufficient to allow a progressive loss of altitude throughout the manoeuvres or sequence. Even the Winjeel with 450 hp had to be climbed to nearly 10,000 ft to allow a ten-minute aerobatic sequence.

The manoeuvres themselves must be adjusted also.

- If the engine has no collector tank for limited inverted flight, the engine would cut from fuel starvation as soon as negative g was sustained. (If it didn't cut, the engine would soon be starved of oil anyway.) To perform a slow roll in this aircraft you would have to be ready for an engine cut halfway through and close the throttle so that the engine didn't over-speed when the fuel supply returned. A float-type carburettor would cut the fuel supply to the engine as soon as positive g was removed. Also, there is a danger of stalling if the pilot tries to sustain inverted level flight with the engine stopping.
- A roll-off-the-top would require a steep dive, very high entry speed and loss of altitude, a high-g pull-up and a downward path to allow an aileron roll to level-flight without having to sustain negative g.

- Aircraft with a limited inverted fuel supply would then be limited by a loss of oil pressure after 30 seconds or so of inverted flight or when the oil pressure dropped suddenly. Inverted flight is difficult enough without having to monitor the oil pressure gauge. Getting to know the aircraft and counting a safe number of seconds is easier than monitoring instruments.
- Induced drag also plays an important role. An aircraft with straight wings, high wing loading and low aspect ratio (therefore the span loading is high, i.e. the weight is carried over a small wingspan) and large square wingtips, may be fast but will lose performance when manoeuvring at high angles of attack.
- Aircraft with a high wing or longer span tend to have a reduced rate-of-roll. Incidentally, the restricted rate-of-roll is a major limitation in being able to escape from a mishandled manoeuvre. For example, if the nose is allowed to drop too far during the second half of a barrel roll then the only recovery is to roll to the nearest horizon and pull out. People who have rolled large transport aircraft carried this enormous risk as they were unable to quickly roll to level and may not have been able to generate enough drag to contain the dangerous build-up of airspeed. (Imagine if the nose of the Boeing 707 had dropped during the second half of that famous barrel roll.)
- Aircraft with cambered aerofoils and positive angle of incidence require a large attitude change and a pronounced forward stick position to maintain level inverted flight. Many basic aerobatic trainers have limited forward stick available for negative *g* manoeuvres and outside turns. Power and airspeed need to be maintained to be able to hold the inverted position.
- Aircraft with dihedral are less stable in inverted flight, so more effort is required to keep the wings level and the aircraft balanced.

Don't be deterred by any of this. It simply requires that the type of manoeuvre and the technique for each is adjusted to suit the capabilities of the aircraft – as they should be – and the type of aircraft is chosen to suit the style of the individual pilots.

The Use of Trim

As discussed, the essence of aerobatic flying and energy management is developing a feel for the onset of buffet, being aware of stick force and position as a guide to an impending stall, and noticing control loads and wind noise as a guide to engine RPM and airspeed.

The development of this sensitivity is adversely affected if the aircraft is constantly re-trimmed to remove out-of-trim stick forces. As a general rule, most properly designed aerobatic aircraft have only a small trim change with changing airspeed so that the out-of-trim forces are not excessive over the operating envelope of the aircraft. In this case, it is preferable to trim the aircraft at an airspeed corresponding to cruise at maximum continuous power and leave it set.

Any reduced airspeed (increased angle of attack) will be reflected in the necessary pull-force. Similarly, speeds above this will be indicated by the push-force required.

Trim (out-of-trim force) is a very valuable reference for flying by feel and, therefore, for developing a sensitivity for aerobatic manoeuvring. With this feel we can also spend more time looking outside. We are now flying by *instinct* rather than flying by *numbers*.

The Use of Power

Power Control and Care of the Engine

Fixed-Pitch Propeller

Engine handling with a fixed-pitch propeller is crucial to avoiding an RPM over-speed on the down-side of manoeuvres – especially the loop, stall turn and perhaps the barrel roll. The RPM increase is the result of a high power throttle position and increasing airspeed. The RPM can be contained in one of two ways:
• by retarding the throttle; or
• by applying g and using the increased induced drag to contain the increasing airspeed.

Some aircraft are more prone to overspeed than others. You will become familiar with the precautions needed for your aircraft.

Constant-Speed Propeller

The constant-speed propeller is far less prone to overspeed, although it can happen. When increasing the power too suddenly while the airspeed is increasing rapidly and there is no aerodynamic resistance to high RPM, the governor may not prevent the RPM limit being exceeded. Avoiding the momentary overspeed simply requires normal restraint on the rate of throttle increase.

Also, a loss of oil pressure (e.g. if the engine stops or by being inverted beyond the time limits of the oil system) reduces the control of the governor and an over-speed can result. For this reason, some aerobatic aircraft have a special propeller which moves to full coarse pitch when the oil pressure drops – thereby preventing an overspeed. (Propellers of single-engined aircraft normally go to full fine pitch).

Torque and Slipstream

As well as managing energy, the use of power has an enormous effect on control-lability at low airspeeds. We are used to high airspeed with stiff controls and high g. We are used to low airspeed with light controls and low g. Now we need to con-sider the unusual combination of low speed, sloppy ailerons, high power, powerful elevators and rudder, high torque, high yawing moments, all in an aircraft with relaxed stability (so that it is highly manoeuvrable).

When we are considering low airspeed, we are now talking of airspeeds at and well below the stalling speed of the aircraft. *How so?*

The stalling speed is the speed in level flight at which the aerofoil reaches its critical angle of attack – its stalling angle. Stalling speed is determined by a particular aircraft's weight, power and configuration. If we are not in level flight, the angle of attack can be anything we make it. We can reach the stalling angle at twice the stalling speed by applying $4g$. Conversely, we can fly at half the stalling speed and stay below the critical angle of attack if we are maintaining less than $1g$. At $+0.5g$ (½ weight so ½ lift required) we can fly at ¼ of the stalling speed (V_2) and we still won't stall the wing. At $0g$ we won't stall at all – even at zero airspeed. However, all of these situations involve a changing flightpath and are transitory. We can't return to $1g$ flight until the airspeed is back above V_S and we must have sufficient altitude to enable this to happen – for the aircraft to accelerate and then apply g to recover from the dive.

Let's look at a practical example. An aircraft such as the Pitts Special is able to roll around a vertical flightpath and rotate in roll at zero airspeed due to the torque reaction of its relatively powerful engine. At zero forward speed there is little aerodynamic resistance to yawing. It can pause at the top of a vertical climb and can rotate in yaw because of the powerful slipstream effect over the rudder and the low directional stability.

Engine/Propeller Stoppage

In many aircraft, especially with fixed-pitch propellers, the engine may stop due to reversed airflow in stall turns and tailslides. Some will stop in a spin. Many have limited inverted flight time before the engine will stop due to interruption of fuel supply or loss of oil pressure. It is not a serious problem

If the engine stops, close the throttle so that there is no risk of overspeed when it restarts. If the engine does not start as the aircraft accelerates, or if the propeller remains stationary (some aircraft require a very steep dive before it will begin rotating), continue diving as altitude permits. The Tiger Moth needs an almost vertical dive. In this event, simply engage the starter (with the throttle closed). The rotation will bring the propeller blades into a positive angle of attack and the engine will quickly restart.

Slipperiness

Most of the aircraft we fly at training schools are *draggy* with a fixed undercarriage and perhaps external bracing. The newer generation of composite-structure, high-performance aircraft are another 'kettle-of-fish'. They are slippery (aerodynamically *clean*) with retractable gear and they are highly powered. They are stressed for aerobatics but there is no trainer. Converting to one of these types is as significant a step as the initial aerobatic training. Special-to-type (type-specific) training is essential for these aircraft.

Chapter 5

Preparation for Aerobatics

When you decide to learn aerobatics, approach it like any other training course and consider all aspects, including cost.

Don't accept an invitation for a friend to show you how it's done – not even a single manoeuvre. Go with a qualified and current instructor, in an approved aircraft, at a safe altitude, with proper preparation and briefing. Accept nothing less. So many pilots and passengers have refused to fly again or to learn aerobatics because they have had a scary experience with an inexperienced pilot showing off.

Save for, and conduct a scheduled programme of instruction, and fly frequently until the manoeuvres become almost second nature.

Where to Learn

Choosing an Aerobatic Training Aircraft

We have discussed the features of an aerobatic aircraft. For training, your choice may be limited. For initial training and for carrying a passenger later, it is comforting to have a side-by-side seating arrangement. For progression to club or competition aerobatics or formation flying, the tandem configuration is better. For other than the very basic manoeuvres, choose an aircraft that offers at least a limited time inverted.

There are many advantages to choosing an aircraft with control columns (joysticks) rather than the control wheel. The stick operates in the logical sense in all directions whereas the yoke has to be rotated. The stick is more directly geared and you can exert more direct force, more quickly. The stick leverage allows better control. The hand can be rested on the thigh during high-g manoeuvres so they are less tiring. The hand does not slip and there is less tendency to apply aileron under g as there is with a yoke.

It is important to fly with one hand on the control column and the other on the throttle. There are occasions when the power has to be quickly applied or removed. Having said that, some aircraft do sometimes require the strength of both hands to achieve full control deflection.

An aircraft with a constant-speed propeller is much easier to manage than a fixed-pitch propeller which tends to over-speed in some manoeuvres. An aircraft with a throttle quadrant allows the hand to be rested on a firm surface under high g so there is no tendency for the hand to drop off the lever – and with support for the hand, it is possible to make more subtle changes than with the unsupported, plunger-type throttle.

A low-wing or mid-wing aircraft will offer a better field-of-view when manoeuvring and probably offer a higher rate-of-roll.

Biplanes offer advantages and disadvantages depending on their aerofoils, controls and power. A Pitt's Special is very different to a Tiger Moth.

Most aerobatic aircraft have a tailwheel configuration and mostly a fixed undercarriage. It should have two accelerometers – one of which should not be resettable (alternatively, it should have an electronic flight recorder). Choose an aircraft that is close in handling and performance to the one you will fly later. If you have a high-performance sports aircraft which is *slippery,* there is little point training in a Stample or a Stearman.

Check the cockpit ventilation if you are flying in a hot climate. There is a real risk of heat stress and dehydration. Open cockpits are fun on a warm day.

Choosing an Instructor

Attitude is everything. Age does not matter nor does total experience. It is the ability to teach and the ability to demonstrate consistent, safe manoeuvres that you are seeking. Find an instructor who loves flying, loves aerobatics, and loves to teach – if you can. They are rare but worth seeking.

Choosing a School

The school is less important than the instructor and the aircraft but check how well the training and the maintenance is managed and how they present and look after their aircraft.

Aerobatic Area

No matter how good your lookout, you can't adequately cover an area sufficiently well during an aerobatic sequence, especially if you are learning or teaching. If possible, choose a training area which has a dedicated aerobatic area with controlled access – so you know you are the only one in it. There's nothing more disconcerting than meeting another aircraft as you go over the top of a loop or when you are half-way though a spin entry.

Parachutes

Some countries, including the United States, require the wearing of parachutes. In other countries they are optional. If you do wear one, ask to be shown the packing date, how to fit the harness correctly and how to use it. Treat it carefully. Do not use it as a cushion on the ground and don't leave it in the sun. Ask also for instruction on emergency egress in flight and practise the procedure as regularly as you fly.

Self-Evaluation/Preparation

Medical Fitness

Aerobatics can be strenuous. You need average medical and physical fitness or you will feel the strain. Don't fly with any illness, no matter how slight – no head-cold, no flu symptoms, no nausea. Ask your doctor if there is any condition about which you are unsure. Also, if you are using medication, ask about its acceptability for flying.

Don't fly with a hang-over – ever. It lowers your tolerance to g, to roll rates, to disorientation and to dizziness. It affects your mental processing speed and ability to concentrate. It also leaves you dehydrated, unrested and unrefreshed.

Physical Fitness

You don't need to be an athlete for aerobatics – at least not until you reach the competitive stage. At the beginning, normal fitness is fine, but fresh air and regular exercise will sharpen your senses, brain function and tolerance to g. As, I think, Ayrton Senna once said, '*the best exercise for Grand Prix drivers is Grand Prix driving*'. It's the same with aerobatics. The manoeuvres themselves, regularly practised, provide aerobatic exercise for the total mind and body. Having said that, moderate aerobic exercise improves alertness, tolerance to g, self esteem and the ability to learn. *What more can one say?*

Hardening

The best way to build a tolerance for aerobatics is to do aerobatics. There is no other way to replicate the stress, g, roll rates, vibrations, sensations and visual cues.

Sleep

Fly only after normal rest. Aerobatics after a late-night (or early-morning) party are not fun. Coffee is not a cure.

Diet

Before flying, eat a light breakfast and avoid greasy food – until you are acclimatised to aerobatics. Toast or cereal is good. Energy foods such as muesli bars and carbohydrates are also good. You will be burning energy. Some people like fruit and yoghurt but some find it unsettling. You know yourself. Drink plenty of water.

Mental Preparation

Read about flying and aerobatics. Sit in the aircraft and imagine the manoeuvres – especially after the first lesson. Be able to quickly read the airspeed, altitude and g.

Once you have established a basic sequence, rehearse it in your mind regularly, down to the minutest detail of where you are going to look, what power you are going to set and what entry speeds you will be looking for. Try to do it in real time – that is, the rate at which it will actually happen in flight. Alan Jones, the Australian world driving champion, rehearsed so well that when he was actually racing, it was as it he was observing his body driving the car and he was able to concentrate on tactics and assessing the track – '*looking through the window of his helmet*' was how he described it.

Many competition pilots do a *rain dance*. They walk through the manoeuvres as they rehearse their sequences on the ground. Learn speeds, power settings, attitudes and limitations by heart. A cue card is OK between sequences but it's far better to learn the routine by heart – like a choreographed dance routine. Imagine Nureyev reading his steps from a card. Aerobatic routines, even basic ones, are no different.

Emergency procedures should be practised until they are automatic. Escape/egress procedures should be demonstrated and practised if you are going to wear a parachute. Ask your instructor about baling-out during a spin.

Recency

Recency describes how recently and how regularly you have flown. When planning your programme try to arrange your time and resources so you can fly regularly and fairly frequently. Ideally, take a continuous period of a week or so, and fly every day.

Once you have completed your initial training maintain recency by flying your routine at least every month or so – more frequently for advanced sequences. If you cannot fly for an extended period then return to aerobatic flying incrementally – i.e. a flight of wing-overs, steep turns and stalls, followed by the basic manoeuvres before you return to a full sequence. If the period is protracted then the safe option is to fly with a safety pilot (an aerobatic instructor) for the first sortie and refresh any aspect about which you are uncertain. Even a ground briefing helps considerably. Know the *HASELL* checks – at least forwards:

H	Height	sufficient to recover by 3,000 ft AGL – or as approved.
A	Airframe	undercarriage, flaps – as required – trim for max cruise IAS
S	Security	harness tight, headset secure, no loose objects, no sharp objects
E	Engine	fuel on and contents, boost pump on, carb heat cold, mixture rich, set maximum continuous RPM or full fine
L	Location	not over built-up area, not over cloud, not over water, clearly defined horizon, note sun position, note direction to home or landing area, clearance or clear of Controlled Airspace. Pick prominent features. Within gliding distance of a suitable landing area.
L	Lookout	wing-overs and clearing turns as required. Check your blind spots

- Check whether your aircraft requires carb heat for stalling and spinning practice.
- Recall the aircraft's recommended speeds and any applicable limitations.
- Recall the manoeuvres, your flight sequence and altitude/area boundaries.

Clothing

Flying Suit

It is more comfortable to wear a flying suit or clothing without a tight waist band. Also the flying suit allows you to safely stow pencils, keys etc. (which really would be better left on the ground). Underclothing should be comfortable and of natural fibre. Be careful to avoid fuel spills on your clothes during the pre-flight. It seriously irritates the skin when you perspire. The smell during flight is also unsettling.

Shoes

Soft, flexible shoes are preferable, with no tread. Tread picks up stones from the tarmac and also can restrict movement of the feet over the floor of the cockpit when applying full rudder and can interfere with centralising the rudder.

Gloves

Gloves are valuable as they grip the plastic of the controls and trim wheel. Your hands will also be sweaty and slippery.

Scarf/Headband

It is very handy to have a sweat band or a cotton scarf that you can use to wipe your forehead and eyes – alternatively you may use the fabric back of the gloves.

Headset Security

A fabric or leather helmet keeps the earphones in place and also captures sweat. Alternatively a cat's collar (it has an elasticised segment) can be attached to a normal headset and functions well as a chin-strap. Route the headset lead through your harness to avoid interference with the controls. Make sure the kneepad doesn't interfere with full and free travel of the control column.

Hats and Sunscreen

The effects of radiation should not be underestimated. Wear a soft hat and sunscreen – but keep it away from your eyes. Fly early morning or late evening in summer.

Sunglasses

Glare can be distracting. Quality sunglasses are invaluable to remove glare and to improve visibility, but ensure they are properly restrained and that the frames do not significantly interfere with your field-of-view.

Secure the glasses with an elastic headband or attach them to the headset frame. Alternatively for those of us who wear corrective lenses, an additional set of anti-glare goggles with a headband can be attached over the top of standard glasses and without interfering with the field-of-view.

Pre-Flight Inspection

Be very thorough with all pre-flight inspections – a school aircraft may have received harsh treatment.

Loose Objects

Don't add to the collection by carrying unnecessary pens, pencils and coins into the aircraft. It is amazing how many aircraft have been lost due to jammed controls arising from a mis-placed loose object. If you drop something, discontinue aerobatics until you locate it. If the aircraft has undergone maintenance be doubly careful to inspect the cockpit and rear fuselage. Tools could have been left inside. If you carry out maintenance on an aerobatic aircraft please account for all tools before signing-off the work.

Strapping-In

Aerobatic aircraft will have a four- or five-point harness, perhaps also with an additional lap-strap. The five-point harness should be locked and tightened as follows:

- Loosen all straps.
- Close and lock the buckle.
- Tighten the lap straps so that they press down and retain the pelvis above the hip joint. This ensures that the skeleton is firmly attached to the aircraft.
- Tighten the crutch strap and tuck away the loose end under your thigh.
- Tighten the shoulder straps to remove any slack but not so tight that you cannot swivel your head and shoulders. You should be able to see the fin out of the corner of your eye. Ensure that the stick is not fouled and that it won't unlatch the lever of the lap buckle.
- Attach and adjust the additional lap-strap harness.

Some higher-performance aircraft have a ratchet on the harness to securely hold the lower abdomen. Some have double lap straps. Some aircraft also have a negative-*g* strap on the rudder pedals or even ski-boot-type attachments to retain the feet during negative *g* manoeuvres. Fit the helmet or headset and connect the lead. Try to route it so that it will not float around during manoeuvres and cannot interfere with the control column. Stow any loose objects.

Preparatory Flying

Refresh your visual flying technique and familiarity with steep turns, stalling, high- and low-speed handling and visual lookout. Refresh the attitudes and power settings for the various flightpaths.

Disorientation

If you have flown recently and a sensible, progressive aerobatic training programme is being followed, you will have no problem with disorientation. Always insist on a clearly defined horizon and stay well clear of cloud. If you do 'lose the place' during manoeuvres, roll to the nearest horizon, and settle down for a while in straight-and-level flight.

Chapter 6

Aerobatic Manoeuvres

Fore-warned is fore-armed

You can't fly by numbers and you cannot learn aerobatics from a book but you can learn what to expect, what to avoid and how best to prepare. As a result, airborne time is more productive and the retention of the training is improved.

Maximum Performance Turning

A maximum performance turn on the buffet playing bank against pitch attitude and thrust against airspeed is an art and a quality that an aerobatic pilot must acquire (in fact, all pilots should acquire).

Description

Maximum performance turning is the ability to manoeuvre in the most efficient way at any speed. It requires the anticipation to increase thrust as *g* is applied, to be sensitive to stall warning cues, and to be able to sustain the aircraft at the point of buffet. At this stage the pilot should be able to be looking outside the aircraft and adjusting the pitch attitude by maintaining the back pressure and temporarily adjusting the bank.

Piloting Technique

Set maximum continuous power and trim the aircraft in straight-and-level flight. Roll into the turn (aileron and rudder) and apply full power. Increase the back pressure and bank angle slowly. Cross-check the attitude and the airspeed until the aircraft is maintaining airspeed at the point of buffet. Note this attitude, speed and load factor. Raise the nose attitude by reducing bank and allow the airspeed to reduce. Reduce back pressure to maintain slight buffet – short of the stall.

Increase the bank and lower the nose and allow the airspeed to increase. Increase the back pressure to maintain the edge of the buffet until you are back to the attitude and speed with which you began.

Points of Airmanship

Keep looking outside, with only brief looks at the ASI, altimeter and accelerometer.

The Wing-Over

Description

The wing-over is a very easy manoeuvre to perform but a very difficult manoeuvre to define – in that it can be almost anything you want it to be.

It can be a climbing manoeuvre, a descending manoeuvre, a turning manoeuvre, a tight manoeuvre or a loose manoeuvre; it can have high angle of bank, low angle of bank, high *g*, low *g*, high power or low power.

We will begin with a set-piece wing-over, through 90° and then 180°, both to feel the characteristics of the aircraft and also to train ourselves where to look and when to look – for what references. Having mastered this, we will then use a variety of wing-overs to align the aircraft with a ground reference and to set the attitude and airspeed for entry into the next aerobatic manoeuvre.

The wing-over is the easiest, most pleasant to fly, and yet useful manoeuvre available in the repertoire.

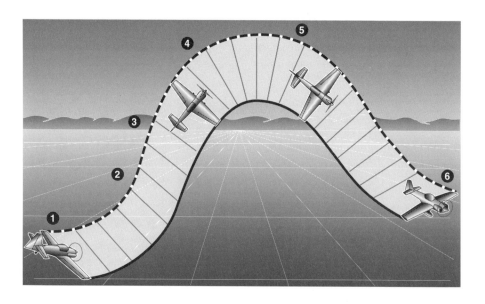

Piloting Technique

Following the normal HASELL check, we'll find a line feature on the ground. When I say a line feature, I mean, a prominent road, railway line, runway or whatever, something that has a reasonable length in a straight line. Position the aircraft at 90° to this line, and we'll use it as a guide. We don't have to be exact nor make corrections for wind, but it is nevertheless a very useful guide for alignment, orientation and position.

1. To enter the first wing-over, we'll establish the aircraft in level flight with maximum continuous power, at around 4,000 feet, AGL.

   As we approach at right angles to a line feature, clearly visible on the right, we'll lower the nose, allow the aircraft to accelerate to V_{NO}, then gently pull up into a straight climb, until the nose is about 15° to 20° above the horizon.

2. Our plan is to enter a right-hand wing-over so that when we come down the other side, we are aligned with the line feature on the ground. Positive pull-up.

3. Now the next important thing is to visually scan – by looking ahead, then looking right, making sure it's clear, and then looking down to the line feature.

4. Roll to a bank angle of 90°, stop the roll, maintain the back pressure at 2*g* or so, and gently pull the nose around the horizon. Be ready to relax the back pressure slightly if the buffet begins. Of course, the nose will also be dropping through the horizon. Allow this to happen.

5. As it goes down and through the horizon, we should be approaching alignment with the line feature, relaxing the back pressure, rolling off the bank to wings-level and then applying slow forward pressure to hold the nose in the entry attitude for the next manoeuvre as the aircraft accelerates back towards V_{NO} – aligned with the line feature.

6. Obviously, we can raise the nose and go through the whole procedure again. It's a very valuable exercise to do alternate wing-overs, left and right, left and right, in a figure-of-eight pattern, using a line feature or features.

The wing-over through 180° is equally simple provided the nose attitude is high before rolling on the bank and provided the pilot plays the back pressure sensitively through the pitching phase of the manoeuvre.

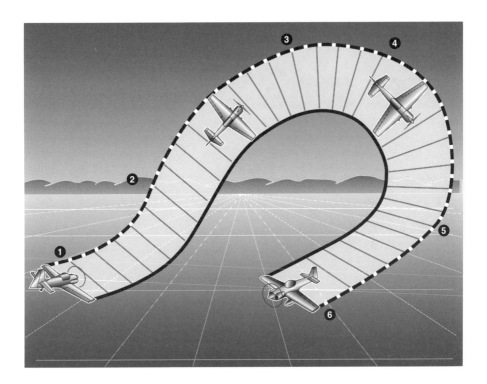

1. (While it appears simple and safe, it can be dangerous near the ground due to the energy loss in the first part of the manoeuvre). Enter the manoeuvre in the same way as before, but judge how much additional airspeed (energy) you may need to complete the wing-over and then be in a position to enter the next aerobatic manoeuvre.

2. Raise the nose well above the horizon and maintain the back pressure as you roll.

3. Roll to 90° of bank or more and now play the back pressure, buffet and bank angle so that you will be rolling out in line with the feature with the nose below the horizon and the aircraft accelerating.

4. Allow the nose to fall through the horizon. Help it along if you need to by maintaining the back pressure and adjusting the bank angle.

5. Anticipate the roll–out and relax the back pressure and even apply some forward pressure to allow the aircraft to accelerate to the entry speed for the next manoeuvre.

6. Try to be precise with the alignment, attitude and airspeed on completion of the wing-over.

These gentle wing-overs are performed with the power set at maximum continuous. As you become competent you may use full power and even idle to achieve the change of direction, attitudes and airspeed control that you want from the manoeuvre. As was said, the wing-over can be anything we want it to be.

OK, let's be a little bit more adventurous. This time, we'll run in at 90° to the line feature, as before, lower the nose, accelerate to V_{NO} and leave the pull-up a little later than before. We'll pull up a little more firmly, say $+3g$, and apply full power. Maintain the back pressure until the nose is about 30° above the horizon, look left, look down at the line feature, roll left to perhaps 120° or until the wings are at right angles to the line feature and pull the aircraft's nose around the corner, again maintaining about $+3g$. Hold the buffet. As the nose comes down through the horizon, anticipate alignment with line feature and roll the wings level. Apply slight forward pressure, accelerating downwards until we have entry speed and entry attitude for the next manoeuvre, which may be a barrel roll or a loop. Watch the propeller RPM as you accelerate.

Points of Airmanship

We have spent so much time describing what is a simple manoeuvre because it is the foundation for all manoeuvring and for the development of feel, anticipation, coordination and judgement. It also is the means for developing a workcycle of looking out and looking where you're going to be going.

The Chandelle

The chandelle (*candle*) is identical to the first part of the wing-over but seeks to make maximum use of the change of airspeed to achieve the greatest altitude gain and change of direction. Thus, in its own way, it is a positioning and set-up manoeuvre for a subsequent entry.

It is particularly good for positioning for a stall or spin entry. You choose the priority of altitude, direction or minimum airspeed to complete the chandelle.

The Aileron Roll

Description

The aileron roll differs from aircraft to aircraft, depending on the roll-rate that can be achieved. In a high-performance aircraft, the aileron roll is almost an instantaneous roll around the aircraft's longitudinal axis. Some aircraft can roll at more than 400°/second. Therefore, if the roll is begun at high airspeed, they can complete one or even several rolls before the momentum is lost and the flightpath descends.

For a typical aerobatic training aircraft, the roll-rate is more likely to be from 60° to 90° per second. Because of this reduced roll-rate (and lower airspeed, momentum and thrust), it's necessary to have the nose raised a reasonable distance above the horizon when we commence the roll so that the aircraft's flightpath and momentum is upward through the first half of the roll and not too far downward during the second half.

Piloting Technique

The easiest way to conduct the aileron roll is to enter in the same way as a wing-over. From maximum cruise, gently lower the nose, allow the aircraft to accelerate to about $2.5 \times V_S$, and then raise the nose symmetrically until the instrument coaming is on the horizon (a normal climb attitude).

1. At this point, 'check' the pitching motion, that is, *freeze* the attitude momentarily, and then smoothly apply full aileron deflection in the direction of roll (without applying forward or back pressure) and add a small amount of rudder – in the direction of the roll – to balance any yaw due to aileron deflection.

2. At the wings-vertical position, maintain the aileron deflection but make sure to relax any back pressure.

3. At the inverted position, relax any back pressure that may be there but don't push forwards more than slightly. Maintain the roll-rate. There is a tendency to relax the aileron pressure at this point and the aircraft will stagger through the last half of the manoeuvre.

4. With 90° to go, again simply maintain the aileron with a little pro-rudder to balance. Don't try to hold up the nose with large rudder deflection (we'll do that later – in the slow roll).

5. The nose will have dropped to the straight-and-level attitude or may be slightly lower, in which case we'll make an adjustment to the entry attitude for the next roll. Later we'll apply a little back pressure for the last 45° of the roll.

6. If the nose is a little low, it is of no matter. It is a useful guide to the entry attitude that should be used next time. Adjust it by the same amount.

At this stage of your training, don't worry about the nose falling through the manoeuvre or about forward pressure on the control column. Simply allow the aircraft to roll through 360° and centralise the controls as you come back to wings level.

Make the initial rolls opposite to the direction of engine rotation, so that the torque of the engine assists the roll. Later, we'll roll in the opposite direction and accept the reduced roll-rate. US horizontally opposed engines rotate clockwise when viewed from the cockpit, so left-handed manoeuvres are easier. UK in-line engines and some US radial engines rotate the other way.

Points of Airmanship

Aileron application should be smooth and full – but not violent. Take about one half second to reach full deflection. Mind your knees and thighs, and knee-pad if you use one. If you are using full aileron warn the instructor or your passenger when you are entering the roll.

The Loop

Description

The loop is very simply a straight pitch through 360° following a nominally circular flightpath. There is positive, but not constant, g throughout.

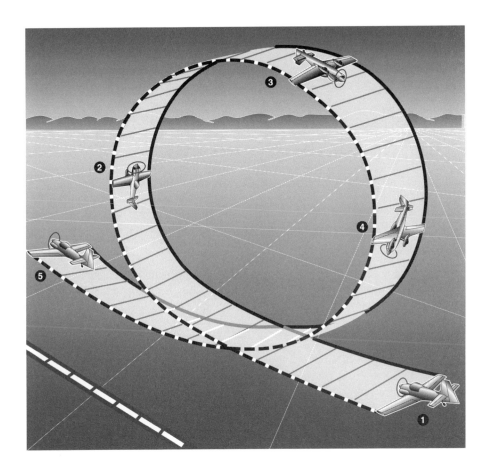

Piloting Technique

1. From now, we will commence all manoeuvres from a 90° wing-over (to the left, if it's side-by-side seating and you're sitting on the left side of the cockpit, to the right if you're in the right-hand seat). Plan the wing-over to arrive in line with your line feature in the attitude for entry to the loop. For most aircraft, this is with the canopy bow on the horizon accelerating towards the recommended entry speed for the loop.

Entry speed will typically be $3 \times V_S$ (or 85–90% of V_{NO}) – but no slower than $2.5 \times V_S$. At $2 \times V_S$ you can theoretically apply $+4g$ which is sufficient for a loop, but remember you will be losing energy as soon as the g is applied.

You'll need to hold forward pressure in the dive to avoid the nose coming up. For aircraft with a fixed-pitch propeller, monitor the engine RPM as the aircraft accelerates. When entry altitude and speed is reached, smoothly and positively apply back pressure, until you have $+3.5$ to $4g$ indicated, and then hold that stick position. Apply full power. If the aircraft is fitted with a yoke, make especially sure that you are pulling symmetrically – as the g can cause you to inadvertently apply aileron as well. Ensure that the instrument coaming is laterally level as it passes through the horizon on the way up. As you approach the vertical, have a quick look, to the left and right, to check that the wings are equally displaced above the horizon.

2. The airspeed is reducing quite rapidly now. You'll need to increase right rudder pressure, because you still have relatively high power and low and reducing air speed – just like a normal climb. Don't look inside, though.

3. At this point, tilt your head right back until you can see the far horizon inverted through the canopy. Maintain the back pressure (the same stick position) but feel for any buffet. There's a tendency to slacken at this stage. If you feel the onset of slight buffet, slightly relax the back pressure to maintain the pitch rate.

4. Be conscious of keeping the wings level over the top of the loop and keeping some right rudder applied. Allow the aircraft to come through the horizon inverted and to accelerate on the downward side. If you have relaxed the back pressure through the top of the loop, reapply back pressure or return the control column back to where it was when you went into the loop. Remember: *feel* your way.

5. As the aircraft accelerates, reduce the right rudder. Pick up your line feature and adjust the bank, if necessary, to pull the nose of the aircraft along the line feature. Monitor the RPM and airspeed during the last 90° of the loop and control the speed with *g*. That is, be prepared to go to maybe +4.5*g* to keep the airspeed from increasing too quickly and to avoid excessive loss of altitude.

 As in a steep turn, there is no better feeling than flying through your own wash.

Note altitude and airspeed and exchange speed for height via a climb or wing-over. Continue to the climb attitude and complete a wing-over, through 90°, back to your pre-loop entry conditions.

At this stage, relax in straight-and-level flight for a few moments, think about the manoeuvre, discuss it with your instructor and then start the exercise again. When you become more confident and proficient, you can simply string loops together with 180° wing-overs at either end or even do consecutive loops (the record is several hundred!).

Don't forget the wing-over is not only the means of establishing the entry conditions for the manoeuvre. It's also your opportunity to have a good look around.

The common errors with the loop are:

- not having the wings exactly level as you pull up, thereby off-setting the axis of the loop;
- not applying rudder through the top half of the manoeuvre, allowing the aircraft to yaw/slip/slew slightly and thereby skewing the loop to one side; and
- not applying the g positively or confidently enough at the beginning, or not applying sufficient g, in which case, the first third of the loop is very elongated and the aircraft won't have sufficient energy to fly through the top of the manoeuvre. It will wallow and fall over the top.

If your aircraft has a yoke instead of a stick then be careful to apply the back pressure symmetrically. Because your arm and hand are grasping one side of the yoke, as the g forces take effect, there is a tendency for your arm to drop and inadvertently apply aileron. Therefore, the pull-up will not be straight. This is a problem with any manoeuvring with this type of control.

Is a Loop Round?

If the aircraft flew a perfectly circular path, and if the aircraft held a constant speed and pitch rate throughout, the load factor would vary from, say, +4*g* at the bottom, through +3*g* when vertical, to +2*g* at the top (gravity modifying the total *g*).

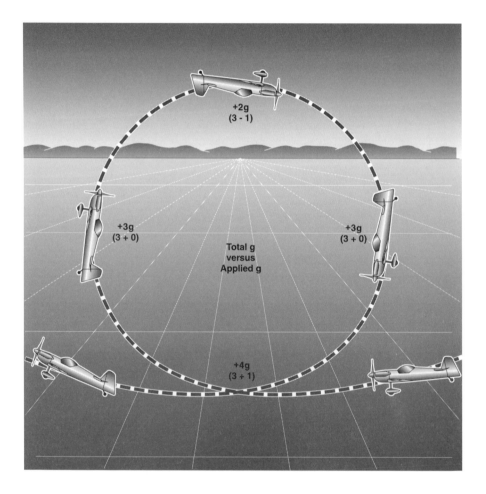

+2g
(3 - 1)

+3g
(3 + 0)

+3g
(3 + 0)

Total g
versus
Applied g

+4g
(3 + 1)

A circular path could also be followed if, as the speed varied, the pitch rate varied in proportion. This is basically what we are trying to do – without having any indicator in the cockpit. Load factor is a measure of speed and pitch rate, so is a guide, but we can't be flying around looking at the instruments as we continuously vary the pitch rate to adjust the load factor to correspond with the airspeed!

However, there is a practical solution. A nominally circular loop can be achieved by having a set entry speed and attitude, and applying a set load factor, say +4g. Then, by holding the stick position constant in that +4g position, the reducing airspeed will result in a reducing pitch rate and load factor which approximates the circular path. It only requires a minor adjustment if the buffet is encountered at the top. At this point the pull force should be slightly relaxed and then reapplied as the aircraft begins to accelerate downhill. As the airspeed builds, a check that the load factor is also building back to +4g will result in a recovery close to the entry altitude. It's simple and it works.

For display flying, some pilots 'play' the back pressure over the top of the loop by extending the inverted part to make up for the otherwise reduced distance travelled at this very low airspeed. They then have more room to position the aircraft on the down side of the loop.

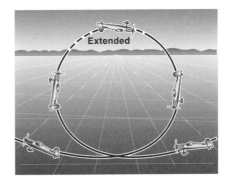

Don't worry about these refinements at this stage. We are not flying in front of a crowd – not yet anyway.

Points of Airmanship

Look ahead of the aircraft and ahead of the pitch-rate. Check the wingtips in the vertical position. After passing the vertical apply some rudder to balance the power at low airspeed. Tilt your head back to find the far horizon, being sensitive to feel the onset of buffet as you do so. The application of g should be firm and positive but not violent – about one second to reach +3.5g. Use the line feature on the down side and adjust the bank and rudder. Engine handling should be smooth and the RPM must be contained.

The Barrel Roll

Description

The barrel roll is a combination of roll, pitch and yaw. The aircraft describes a horizontal spiral through the sky. Imagine a ribbon with the aircraft planform drawn on it at five points.

Then we join one end of the ribbon to the other in the form of a ring or hoop, then obviously, if that stands vertical, we are describing the flightpath of the aircraft through a loop. Note that the aircraft is inverted half-way through the manoeuvre but that the pitch attitude is greatest at the 90° up and down points (one-quarter and three-quarters of the way through the manoeuvre, respectively).

If we were to take the two ends of the ribbon, pull them straight, but twist the ribbon through 360° (it will resist the twist), you will see the planform of the aircraft as it goes through an aileron roll or a slow roll manoeuvre.

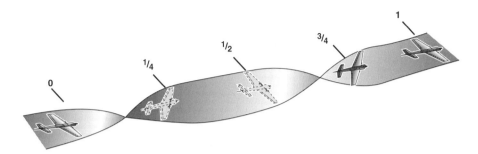

Note that it is inverted half-way through the manoeuvre, and if we started with a slightly climbing flightpath the nose attitude is highest at the wings–vertical point and lowest also at the three-quarter wings–vertical point.

Let's now take the ribbon and displace the ends from the loop until they are half-way between the straight hoop and the straight twist. We now have a manoeuvre that's somewhere between the loop and the aileron roll. You'll see the ribbon describes the horizontal spiral that we discussed. This is the barrel roll. Note that the inverted position is at the highest point of the roll and that the steepest nose-up and nose-down attitudes are at the wings–vertical positions.

Particularly note that the top of the barrel roll is when the aircraft is inverted. It has to be. The only way an aircraft (other than a Harrier which has vectored thrust) can generate centripetal force towards the centre of the roll (which it must have to change the flightpath in that direction) is to use part of the lift force of the wings. The lift generates the centripetal force. You'll find some publications which show the aircraft with the wings vertical at the top of the barrel roll. The argument has gone on since the manoeuvre was invented. But it is a very important error. Mis-understanding the apogee of the roll has contributed to several fatal accidents.

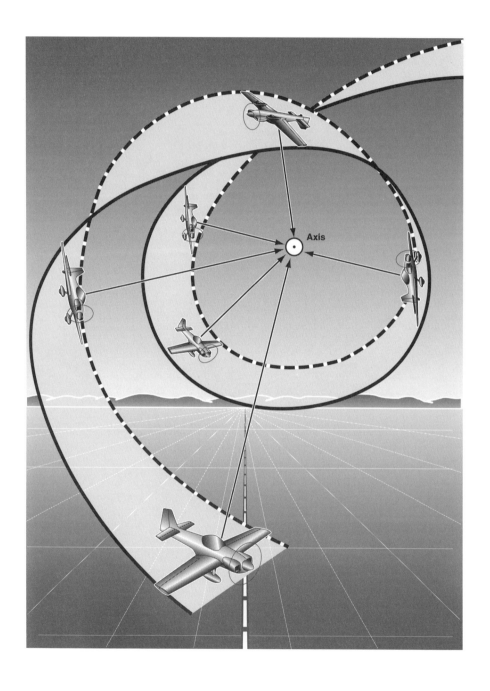

Axis

Note also that the pitch attitude is steepest at the wings-vertical point and lowest at the three-quarter roll wings-vertical position. This has been the cause of confusion with the barrel roll. *The attitude is steepest at the wings-vertical point but the flightpath is still climbing until it reaches the inverted position.* Any attempt to pull the nose down after the wings-vertical point will cause the second half of the roll to bottom out.

If you reach the wings-level, inverted position, with the nose passing through the horizon, there is no way you can complete the roll without 'barrelling-out' of the bottom. It is the greatest cause of problems with the barrel roll and it's also been the cause of many fatal display accidents. Once the nose is committed low and you have a limited roll-rate, then you are a goner.

The wings must be generating lift towards the centre of the roll at all times for the aircraft to change its flightpath in that direction, and the aircraft must climb through the first half of the roll to be able to recover at the entry altitude in the remaining half.

Piloting Technique

To enter the barrel roll, we start with the usual wing-over through 90°. Set the aircraft up 500 feet or so above the entry altitude, at 90° to the line feature, and you'll find it works out more comfortably if you do a left wing-over into a right-hand barrel roll or a right-hand wing-over into a left-hand barrel roll.

There are two ways to select and use a reference for the roll:
* pick a point 60°–90° off the nose in the direction of the roll. This will be the reference for alignment at the inverted position;

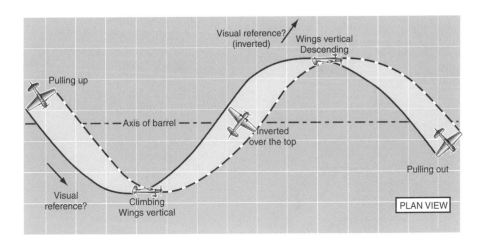

- or pick your normal line feature and exit the wing-over 30°–45° through the axis, planning to be the corresponding angle off-axis in the other direction, as you go over the top.

The latter is an easier method if you have been used to using a line feature.

1. Because the engine torque in most aircraft favours the left roll, we'll plan a right wing-over into a left roll. Raise the nose into the wing-over, look right, roll right, pull the aircraft around the corner and pull through the line feature by about 30°. By this time, the nose will have dropped through the horizon. Continue to pull and roll until you have the canopy bow on the horizon. Stop the roll and allow the aircraft to accelerate to the entry speed.

2. Smoothly apply +2g to +3g and continue the nose through the horizon until the instrument coaming passes through the horizon.

   At this point, introduce about half aileron deflection. You'll need a touch of rudder to balance in the same direction as the applied aileron – but unlike other rolls, *maintain the back pressure.* This is the most important stage of the barrel roll.

3. One could say that the first part is roll and pull, the second part is more roll but less pull, and the last part, increasing pull and less roll.

   Allow the aircraft to then zoom (due to its momentum), and maintain the roll and pitch rates until the aircraft approaches the wings-vertical position.

4. At this point the nose should be well and truly above the horizon. With the reducing airspeed, the roll-rate will tend to reduce, so for the second quarter of the roll, you'll need to increase the aileron deflection and at the same time relax the back pressure a little.

5. The inverted top-of-the-roll position should be equivalent to the inverted top-of-the-loop position, that is, with the canopy bow on the horizon and the instrument coaming still well above the horizon.

   At this reduced airspeed, you'll need slightly more rudder to balance and a little more aileron to keep the roll-rate constant.

6. The aircraft will now start to accelerate on the downward half of the roll: you'll need to reintroduce additional back pressure (yes, back pressure) and slightly reduce the amount of aileron deflection to continue a constant roll-rate through the bottom of the manoeuvre.

7. The increasing back pressure and reducing aileron is the second most important part of a successful barrel roll. It takes some finesse to balance the increase of one with the decrease of the other.

8. As the aircraft accelerates, you can use reduced rudder deflection to balance. The aircraft will roll nicely out on the line feature, pointing 30° or so off-axis – the same way as you did on entry. Your aircraft may have an offset fin or an offset engine to partly counter the torque and slipstream effects. Think about this when planning the manoeuvre.

The barrel roll is a very comfortable and pleasant manoeuvre but difficult to fly accurately and in balance – and therefore is a very good manoeuvre to practise. Ultimately, you'll be able to rest your knee-pad or other soft object on the instrument coaming and leave it there for the duration of the roll, just as Bob Hoover does with his cup of water.

Common Errors With the Barrel Roll

Common errors with the barrel roll are:

- not getting the nose high enough at the beginning, before introducing the aileron;
- allowing the roll-rate to reduce over the top and therefore allowing the nose to become too low at the commencement of the second half of the roll; or
- going from the 90° wings-vertical position to the inverted position while maintaining too much back pressure – thereby pulling the nose across and down and giving an insufficiently high nose attitude to commence the second half of the roll.

The barrel roll can be done with a variety of roll versus pitch ratios. It can be loop-like with very high pitch angles or roll-like with small pitch angles. A typical barrel roll contains 360° of roll and about 40° of pitch (10° nose down to 20° nose-up to 10° nose-down again – a total of 40° traversed). Thus the roll/pitch ratio and rates are nearly ten to one. Start on the easy side by raising the nose to a good 20° or 30° above the horizon and rolling fast rather than slowly. Adjust the ratio of roll to pitch during the last quarter of the manoeuvre.

The combination of aileron and elevator can stretch the 'barrel' from a very large elongated roll not far displaced from the loop, down to a very tight rapid barrel roll, not unlike a curved aileron roll. For most purposes, somewhere in between is a good balance. The 30°–45° off-set from the line feature is a good reference.

Having completed the barrel roll to the left, continue the nose-up through the horizon, into a left-hand wing-over, back to the 90° position.

Eventually we'll go from that left wing-over, into a right-hand barrel roll, into a right wing-over, into a left-hand barrel roll, into a left wing-over and so on. It makes a very nice, flowing sequence. You can, of course, put a loop in the middle there. We'll look at a sequence in the next chapter.

Points of Airmanship

Look out while flying the manoeuvre. You do need a clearly defined horizon. Feel the back pressure and observe the roll-rate. If you do not feel comfortable about the way the manoeuvre is developing, remove all back pressure and roll to wings-level.

The Stall Turn

Description

In very simple terms, the stall turn is a pull-up to a vertical zoom, and before all forward momentum is lost, the aircraft is yawed through 180° into a vertically downward dive. After accelerating to normal flying speed, the aircraft is recovered to level flight. In the process, the aircraft has obviously reversed direction.

There are various combinations and permutations which add various types of roll to the upward and downward segments of the stall turn but we'll stay with the basic manoeuvre. It is a fairly simple manoeuvre and is comfortable to perform. There is little stress on the aircraft or pilot other than in the pull-up and the dive recovery. However, there is a slight feeling of insecurity (a 'pregnant' pause) at the vertical, no airspeed stage but you will soon get used to this if you perform the manoeuvre regularly.

The stall turn is a manoeuvre where the aircraft is pitched to a vertical path and held at $0g$ until well below V_S. The airflow from the propeller allows some control power for the elevators, and more particularly the rudder, and this is used to yaw the aircraft through 180° until it is facing vertically down. Then the aircraft has to be allowed to accelerate in $0g$ flight until it has sufficient airspeed to apply $+3g$ or so for the dive recovery (later you may use a negative g recovery in a competition aircraft). So the stall turn isn't a stall, at all, at all – after all.

Consider for a moment, the aircraft at the top of the zoom at very low airspeed with full power. Full rudder is applied with engine torque assisting or countering the yaw, depending on the direction of the yaw.

All aircraft with US horizontally opposed engines will stall turn left far more easily than right because the engine torque is assisting. Interestingly, there is a rolling moment due to the induced effect of the yaw – which must be countered with gross use of opposite aileron (because of very low airspeed over the surfaces).

Note that we now have full pro-spin controls – but of course, we are nowhere near the stalling angle of attack.

The gyroscopic precession of the engine/propeller combination will cause a nose-up pitching moment as the aircraft yaws left (left yaw causes pitch-up with a clockwise direction of engine rotation – as viewed from the cockpit). Therefore, slight forward control pressure is required to maintain the yawing plane.

The stall turn is a difficult manoeuvre to feel as the airspeed is close to zero and the aircraft behaviour is dominated by the slipstream, torque and prop-wash effects. It is an interesting manoeuvre.

Piloting Technique

The stall turn is identical to the loop for the first 90° of pitch. Same entry, same look-out, same wing-over, same straight pull-up, same full power, checking that the coaming is parallel to the horizon as it passes through.

1. A straight pull-up is critical for the stall turn. Maintain the *g* until you reach the vertical position with reference to the wingtips.

   Go slightly beyond the vertical to allow for angle of incidence. Apply right rudder (usually), as the airspeed reduces, to stay vertically straight.

   With practice, you will have a moment to check that each wingtip is the same distance above the horizon – and therefore the vertical path is straight.

2. At the vertical position, the pilot simply checks the pitching motion and
   holds the aircraft in a climbing flightpath with forward pressure.

Look left for a left–hand stall turn.

3. After a momentary pause, firmly and progressively apply full left rudder. With the left rudder, there will initially be slight reluctance and then the aircraft will start to yaw left. As it does so, the secondary effect of yaw causes the aircraft to tend to roll in the same direction. Thus you'll need left rudder, forward pressure to hold zero *g* and some right aileron to keep the plane of the yaw flat in relation to the vertical axis of the aircraft – and the vertical axis of the aircraft horizontal to the earth. Look at the nose.

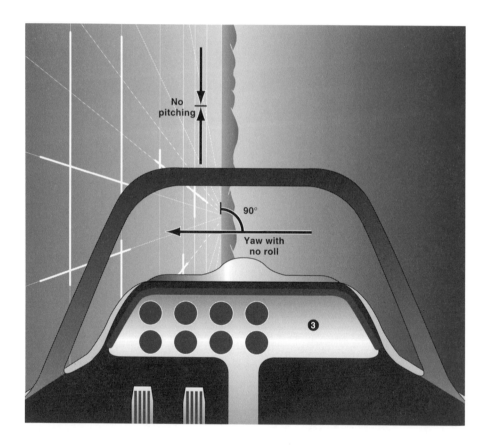

As the nose slices through the horizon, check for verticality and, if necessary, make an aileron input to correct. You may reduce the engine power at this stage but it is not essential. Some aircraft need to have the power reduced for a right-hand stall turn, but optionally for the left. As the aircraft points down, it will want to oscillate like a pendulum as it goes through the nose-down vertical position and until the airspeed builds. You may use the rudder actively to stop this oscillation.

4. You can apply fairly coarse right rudder and then left rudder to check this oscillation. Of course, at this very low airspeed, there is not a great deal of control power.

5. As the aircraft accelerates, check your reference line and smoothly and firmly apply the same amount of back pressure as you would for recovery from the last half of the loop.

In a right-hand stall turn you may need to reduce the engine power as soon as the yaw rate is established. Otherwise the engine effects will resist the yaw.

A stall turn to the right is a little more difficult, because you have the engine resisting you over the top. Same entry on pull-up, look to the right 90° check, introduce some right rudder, while you still have the slipstream effect of the engine, and as soon as the aircraft starts to yaw, slowly and smoothly reduce the power. The aircraft will then slice through the horizon, into the nose-down position and accelerate.

Be careful not to exceed the engine RPM when reintroducing the power.

The stall turn is a pleasant, but less controlled manoeuvre than previous ones, because for a moment, at the top of the manoeuvre, the aircraft is almost stationary, with high power, reduced control power except for the rudder and elevator in the propwash, and no airflow over the ailerons. Thus, you are relying on momentum and then gravity for the aircraft to come out in the right direction.

There is a tendency not to be truly vertical, and in fact, being less than vertical or partially vertical makes it more difficult to yaw with reference to the vertical plane. There is also a tendency, if there is any reverse air flow as the aircraft starts to slide backwards, for it to pitch rather than yaw. Then it becomes what is called a hammerhead, with the nose pitching violently down or over the top.

Points of Airmanship

You really need a clearly defined horizon for the stall turn. The aircraft is in a regime where it could easily depart from controlled flight (large rudder deflections, potentially large aileron deflections, very low airspeed, high power and the aircraft starting to slide backwards). If the aircraft starts to auto-rotate or to tailslide, you must close the throttle, centralise the controls and wait. It can be quite a violent reversal and change of direction. Simply hang on until the aircraft is accelerating downwards and you have normal aerodynamic control restored. If you are worried about tail-sliding then apply rudder but be ready to prevent it going to full deflection and being damaged.

If anything, when pulling up, err slightly past the vertical. It is more comfortable to pitch backwards rather than forwards – if anything goes wrong.

Inverted Flight

Description

Inverted flight is simply flying straight, level and balanced upside-down. However, you must take into account that the aircraft may have a positive rigger's angle of incidence and positive camber.

Inverted attitude

The attitude for inverted flight will be markedly nose-high (above the horizon) probably equivalent to the climb attitude reversed, i.e. canopy bow on the horizon, inverted.

In erect flight, the aircraft is balanced in pitch and the tailplane is rigged, so that there is a down-load on the tailplane. This tends to keep the nose up.

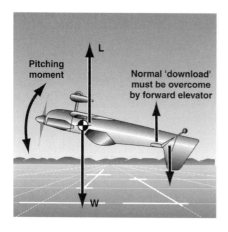

When the aircraft is inverted, this has the result of trying to lower the nose relative to the horizon. Even more forward stick is required, especially at low airspeeds. There may not be enough control power to maintain level inverted flight at airspeeds slower than normal cruise speed.

When inverted, the stalling speed is also increased – as the camber of the aerofoil is contrary to the curvature of the airflow.

Piloting Technique

Rolling to Inverted Flight

1. From a wing-over, accelerate to fast cruise speed, say twice V_S, raise the nose to the climb attitude or slightly higher, 'check' the pitch rate and apply full aileron with a little rudder to balance.

2. Apply some top rudder as the wings pass the vertical and make sure that the positive g is relaxed as the roll is started, and then, after wings-vertical, progressively apply forward pressure until inverted. Progressively release the rudder as the inverted position is reached.

3. Maintain the aileron deflection as you push forward through the vertical. There is a tendency to centralise it. Typically, the inverted flight attitude is with the canopy bow on the horizon. It may take almost full forward stick to maintain inverted flight if the aircraft has a cambered aerofoil and a positive angle of incidence. At this point, all of the dust, dirt and loose particles from the cockpit floor will fall past your eyes. (*Yes, it happens.*) Loose shoulder straps will float in front of your face and the headset lead may snake across your field-of-view.

The *floaters* can be disconcerting but try to concentrate on flying the aircraft and maintain the straight, level and balanced inverted attitude.

Note that the rudder is *not* reversed in inverted flight. All of the controls always work in the same sense – *as viewed by the pilot.* Continue to *step on the ball* (if you have an inverted balance ball).

Also, adverse aileron yaw operates in the same sense – *as viewed by the pilot.* If one wished to enter an inverted turn from inverted flight with an aileron input, say to the left (for a left turn as perceived from the ground), then the adverse yaw (to the right as perceived by the pilot) is, in fact, not adverse to the turn! (It makes a good debate at the 'local'.)

To stay level inverted, maintain the pitch attitude by normal pushing and pulling on the control column.

Similarly, keep the wings level to the horizon as you would normally. Use the rudder to balance by looking into the distance and keeping straight. The balance ball (skid-ball) is one reference that does not work inverted, although aircraft capable of sustained inverted flight will have an inverted skid-ball for this purpose.

Rolling to Erect Flight

Return to erect flight by completing a slow roll or aileron roll. Apply rudder in the same direction as the aileron. This will overcome adverse aileron yaw and help to keep the nose-up through the wings-vertical position. Bring the control column back through neutral so that back pressure is applied for the last 90 degrees.

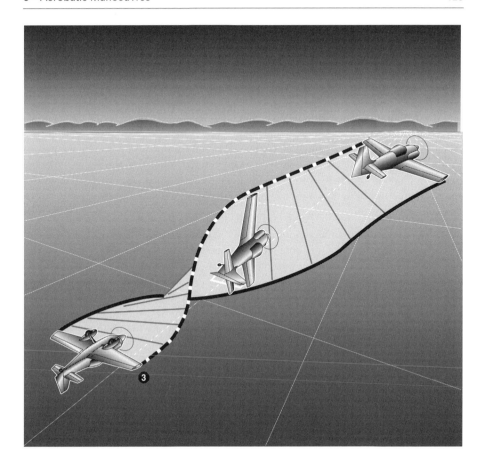

Points of Airmanship

Double-check that your harness and that of your passenger is *completely* tight and secure. Double-check there are no loose objects. Do not enter the roll below the recommended speed. If the aircraft is too slow, the extra amount of forward pressure required to maintain inverted level flight, and the fact that stall speed inverted is likely to be higher than in erect flight, may be sufficient to stall the wing inverted and thus create the possibility of an inverted departure and spin entry. Similarly, a violent application of forward stick approaching the inverted position may cause the same result, or even an outside flick roll.

Check and observe any limitations that apply to your aircraft as far as inverted flight and engine handling is concerned. If the engine coughs, relax the forward pressure immediately and roll to wings-level, closing the throttle at the same time.

The Slow Roll

Description

The slow roll is known as a coordination exercise but, in fact, the control inputs are contrary to almost any other manoeuvre. They are all *crossed-up*. The slow roll used to be deliberately slow as the longer the duration of the roll, the more difficult the coordination, the flightpath control and the achievement of a constant roll-rate. Also, it used to take a long time to fly the full length of the field over which the roll was being performed. Nowadays, the slow roll is only called *slow* because it is slower than the aileron roll (which in most aircraft with limited roll-rate, is done with full aileron deflection). For the slow roll, about half aileron deflection is used.

Note: *slow* does not refer to low airspeed.

More significant than the time taken is that the slow roll follows a nominally level flightpath, whereas the aileron roll is simply a roll using aileron alone, and the flightpath during the roll is not corrected to any great extent – in fact, as we know, it changes from a slightly ascending to a slightly descending path. Further, no negative *g* is experienced in the inverted attitude of the aileron roll, whereas the slow roll passes through the true inverted flight attitude and −1*g*.

In the slow roll, the flightpath is managed throughout to maintain straight-and-level through the knife-edge and inverted stages of the roll. Thus the aircraft changes from positive to negative angles of attack and from balanced flight to high sideslip angles in each direction – while at the same time maintaining a nominally constant rate-of-roll.

A perfect roll would look like this:

However, most aircraft require a slightly raised nose attitude on entry to achieve a level attitude on completion.

Piloting Technique

Before commencing the slow roll, which some would say is a difficult, uncomfortable and unbalanced manoeuvre, we'll firstly explore inverted flight and practise the first half of the roll to the inverted attitude.

The aircraft you fly may be restricted to 30 seconds of inverted flight, due to falling oil pressure. It may be restricted to even less by the lack of an inverted fuel system. Alternatively, it may allow unlimited inverted flight. If it is restricted, you may roll to inverted, hold it momentarily, recognise the attitude and the control positions and then return to erect level flight. To return from inverted to level flight is more difficult than the first half. As the aircraft is rolled, the forward pressure is progressively relaxed until there is none as the aircraft passes the wings-vertical position. Then there is a need for back pressure and some top rudder as the aircraft rolls through 45°, and then reducing rudder as the aircraft reaches level.

1. Next, we'll attempt the complete slow roll. To enter, start with a normal wing-over entry, pulling the nose up until the instrument coaming is at least on the horizon and check (stop the pitching).

In lower-performance aircraft the nose may have to be as high as 20°–30° above the horizon. Smoothly apply half aileron in the direction of roll, and on this occasion, start to introduce opposite, yes, opposite rudder (adverse aileron yaw helps us here).

2. So left aileron, rolling left and because we want to roll around the point, we apply right rudder to stop the nose moving to the left and ease the control column forward.

As the wings approach the vertical position, we'll have almost full right rudder (top rudder) applied to stop the nose dropping, and any back pressure we had will now be neutralised. As we go through the wings-vertical attitude, we'll start to apply progressive forward pressure to hold the nose up.

3. As the roll continues, rudder is progressively reduced so that it is centralised at the inverted attitude.

As the aircraft approaches the inverted attitude there is a tendency to apply insufficient forward pressure. There is also a tendency to reduce the aileron deflection, and so the roll-rate deteriorates while the nose continues to drop.

4. After the inverted position the roll-rate is maintained and progressive (large) left rudder is introduced. This last half is the difficult part, as the aileron has to be maintained, more rudder introduced, and then reduced after wings vertical, and the stick has to move through the trimmed position to progressive back pressure for the last quarter of the roll. It is likely that the airspeed will have decayed during the roll and so more back pressure is required than you would expect to keep the nose up.

If there is a cloud you can use as a reference, simply use rudder and stick as required, to keep the nose in one position as you roll through 360°!

Points of Airmanship

Even though the inverted position is transitory, you will experience all of the effects of negative g $(-1g)$. The same considerations apply. If the engine fails or hesitates, or the oil pressure warning illuminates, relax the back pressure and complete the roll. Close the throttle as you do so. If it 'falls' out, i.e. the nose attitude cannot be maintained when inverted, again relax the forward pressure and roll while closing the throttle. If you are pushing firmly on the control column and you experience any airframe or control buffet, relax at least some of the forward pressure, and accept the altitude loss as you complete the roll. Chances are that the entry speed was too low, or you started the roll a little too soon.

Roll-Off-the-Top (Immelmann Turn)

Description

The roll-off-the-top was developed by a World War I pilot, named Max Immel-mann, as a rapid way of reversing direction without loss of altitude, in the least space, and with minimal loss of energy. Like the gentler chandelle, kinetic energy (*airspeed*) is exchanged for potential energy (*altitude*).

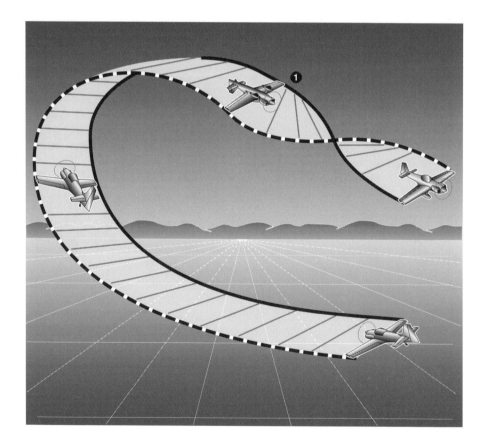

The roll-off-the-top consists of a loop to inverted flight and an aileron roll or slow roll (or even a flick roll) to level flight. Thus the aircraft changes direction quickly.

The term, *slow roll,* is not strictly correct, as there is no intention to roll slowly, but the term is used to describe the fact that in this case, the pilot holds negative *g* briefly while the pitch rate is 'checked' – rather than allowing the nose to drop during the roll. Aircraft with a decent roll-rate will simply roll out, while those with a low rate-of-roll at this low speed will have to be held level during the roll.

For aircraft with limited inverted flight capability, it is far more logical and comfortable to allow the nose to fall through the roll and to roll simply with aileron, coordinated with rudder.

Piloting Technique

The true roll-off-the-top is not an easy manoeuvre. Entry speed and load factors are higher than a loop so that the aircraft has more energy to roll at the top. The aircraft is slow at the start of the roll and almost full forward stick is required to maintain inverted level flight. Full aileron deflection is needed (with possible pronounced adverse yaw), the engine is at high power and as the aircraft rolls, there will be considerable sideslip. This is a regime where an inverted stall and departure from controlled flight is possible unless the aircraft has plenty of energy and control power. Some aircraft may enter an inverted spin from here.

Talk this aspect through with your instructor.

Some references describe an alternative roll-off-the-top with a half barrel roll. This is clearly illogical as it will result in completing the manoeuvre off-line – the axis of a barrel roll being offset from the aircraft direction of flight. However, it can be completed quite pleasantly with a half flick roll.

Points of Airmanship

During the pull-up the aircraft is at high speed and high *g*. Control inputs should be tempered. The roll needs to be started with the nose well above the horizon, and in the knowledge that care is needed.

Half-Roll-and-Pull-Through (Split-S)

Description

The half-roll-and-pull-through is simply that – a half roll to inverted followed by the second half of a loop. The roll can be an aileron roll or a slow roll but it is vital to start the half loop at low airspeed and with a nose-high inverted attitude.

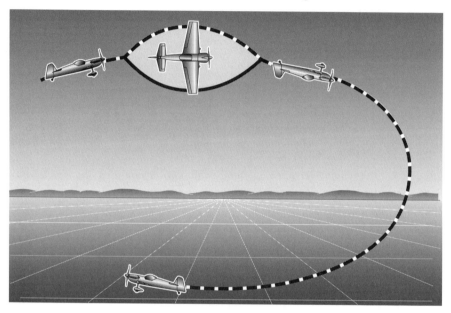

Piloting Technique

The easiest method for the aircraft and the pilot, is to pull-up slightly from below cruise speed to the normal climb attitude, pause, roll to inverted, pause and smoothly apply positive g – being careful to avoid the buffet. Once the g is applied, the airspeed will be contained and as the aircraft accelerates, a normal loop is completed. The throttle can be retarded, or, if necessary, closed once the aircraft is accelerating downhill.

Points of Airmanship

This is a risky manoeuvre if entered with a nose-low attitude. Make a distinct pull-up before the roll. Any excess speed or acceleration in the first quarter of the manoeuvre is dangerous – if in doubt, close the throttle, roll upright and pull out. Conversely, a slow entry or excessive buffet at the beginning can delay acceleration to manoeuvring speed and can actually cause the aircraft to lose more altitude in the manoeuvre. It can stagger rather than fly through the manoeuvre. It is a matter of playing back pressure against increasing airspeed.

Knife-Edge Flight

Description

Unless the aircraft has upward momentum, any manoeuvre requiring 90° of bank will result in a loss of altitude. Whether in sustained straight flight at 90° of bank, or partially through a slow roll or a hesitation roll, there is a need to generate lift from sources other than the wings – otherwise the flightpath will curve downwards. High-performance aircraft with high roll-rates can momentarily raise the nose (upward path), roll rapidly and complete the roll before the flightpath descends below horizontal. For a true horizontal path, though, we have to use other means to sustain the level path.

Vertical wings can contribute nothing to maintaining a level flightpath. Gravity can only be balanced by a side force from the fuselage, fin and rudder (with a contribution from the thrust vector). This requires that the aircraft has sufficient rudder power to hold the nose up (in relation to the horizon) against the directional stability of the aircraft trying to cancel any sideslip. If the rudder power is sufficient to do this, then the aircraft can be made to maintain a high sideslip angle, and the side-force from the fuselage and fin then generates the 'lift' to balance the force of gravity.

The engine also contributes a little. The thrust from the propeller at this high sideslip angle has a component at 90° to the flightpath, as well as the major component along the flightpath.

Some aircraft can sustain this sideslip just enough to complete a rolling manoeuvre. Others, such as the Pitts Special, can fly indefinitely this way.

At such high sideslip angles, there is a dihedral effect too. The lower wing presents greater frontal area to the relative airflow, and unless there is exactly zero lift, there may be a small rolling moment towards erect flight. If the wing has a positive angle of incidence or camber, then the effect is more pronounced.

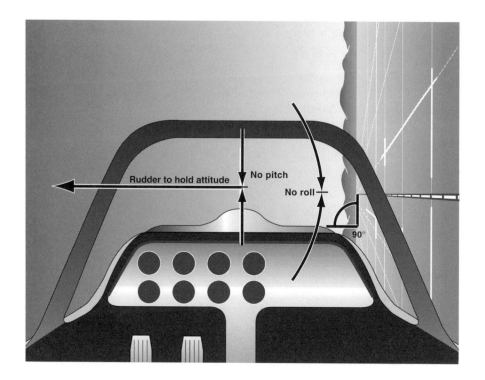

Piloting Technique

The aircraft needs a nose-high attitude corresponding to the attitude for the 90° position before the roll. Then the roll should be done quickly to the wings-vertical position. A large amount of rudder will be required to keep the nose at the equivalent attitude to the entry position. Be sensitive to fin/rudder buffet.

Points of Airmanship

For most aircraft, a reasonable entry airspeed is required so that the side-force is sufficient to maintain level flight. At lower airspeeds, full rudder may be insufficient to hold the nose up and may even stall. Full rudder should only be applied at speeds below V_A.

Hesitation Rolls

Description

The hesitation roll consists of 4, 8 or even 16 hesitations (pauses) during the roll. To be completed in a reasonable space with reasonable airspeed and with distinct pauses, it requires quite harsh control inputs.

It is a *bang, bang*, full aileron, no aileron type of manoeuvre and not particularly pleasant – especially for a passenger. It is much easier in a higher-performance aircraft with high momentum and high rates-of-roll. Adverse aileron yaw is also a difficulty at lower airspeeds.

Piloting Technique

Let's restrain ourselves to a four-point roll. Entry is the same as a slow roll, but full aileron is used and a higher entry speed. (At airspeeds above V_A, which may be necessary for some aircraft, initially use less than full control deflection.) As the aircraft approaches the wings-vertical position, the roll is checked and the nose held momentarily with top rudder. The aileron is suddenly reapplied and the roll continued with forward pressure to hold the nose up as the aircraft approaches the inverted attitude. The roll is again stopped inverted and then aileron is suddenly reapplied until the wings-vertical position. The forward pressure has been replaced with a large amount of top rudder. The last part sees the roll supported by back pressure as the rudder is centralised.

Points of Airmanship

The hesitation roll is relatively straightforward. Concentration is high and lookout is almost impossible to maintain. The aileron inputs are easy but it takes a little practice to coordinate the rudder and elevator inputs.

Flick Roll (Snap Roll)

Description

In the flick roll, the aircraft is caused to depart from controlled flight by stalling one wing and yawing during an accelerated stall. Full rudder, and usually full aileron, assist the rotation. It is effectively a one-turn horizontal spin.

Opposite aileron or, sometimes, normal spin recovery controls are applied to stop the roll after a half or one turn. It is an easy and quite comfortable manoeuvre provided the entry speed is kept low. The aircraft can be damaged by flick rolls at too high a speed, as not only are the g forces higher, the side loads on the fin and rudder are also very high. The best place for a flick roll is from inverted to inverted at the top of a loop when the airspeed is low and decreasing, the flightpath is initially upward, there is altitude to spare, and all the forces are low. It works very well. It is also a fun variation of a roll-off-the-top.

There is also an outside flick roll induced from negative g or inverted flight, rather than a positive g entry.

Piloting Technique

The flick roll, from level flight, is entered from low airspeed (the manufacturer will specify, or at least should recommend, a strict maximum speed for entering a flick roll and note that it is well below V_A). From level flight, some 10 knots or more below the limiting speed, raise the nose to the climb attitude, apply full power and then simultaneously apply full back stick, full rudder and after rotation starts, full aileron in the direction of the roll. You will feel the buffet and the stall of the down-going wing almost immediately. Hold the controls firmly. Apply opposite aileron and rudder, depending on the rate of roll, about 45° before wings-level and release back pressure to unstall the wings. The aircraft will stop rotating very quickly (much quicker than a spin recovery) due to the slipstream from the propeller over the rudder and elevators.

Points of Airmanship

Don't ever exceed the limiting speed and don't enter the manoeuvre if the aircraft is accelerating or descending. Only do it with a clear horizon and don't do it by half measures. The flick roll is a sudden, almost violent, buffet, stall, roll, spin, recover, *'What happened?' 'It didn't hurt, did it?'* sort of manoeuvre.

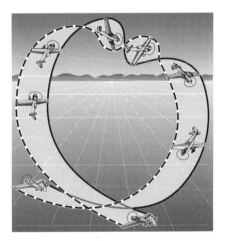

At the top of a loop, it is almost gentle in comparison. This is known as the avalanche or Porteous loop.

Avalanche (Porteous Loop)

Description

The avalanche is also called the Porteous loop after the test pilot who introduced it at the Farnborough air show in the Auster J5F Aiglet. It is easy, safe and quite spectacular from the cockpit, as well as from the ground. It consists of a complete flick roll from the inverted attitude to the inverted attitude at the top of a normal loop.

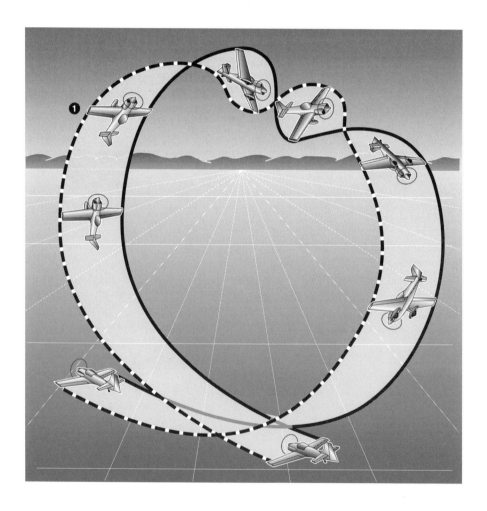

Piloting Technique

Simply enter a loop and when the far horizon comes into sight towards the top of the loop increase the back pressure until the buffet is noticeable and then apply full rudder.

As the aircraft stalls, move the stick fully back. Centralise the stick and stop the roll with opposite rudder as it completes the roll towards the inverted position. The nose will now be below the horizon and it is then very easy to complete the loop.

It takes a conscious effort to pull through the buffet into the stall at the top of the loop. There is a tendency to leave it all too late and to end up steeply nose-down. Start applying excessive back pressure as soon as the far horizon comes into the forward field-of-view.

Points of Airmanship

It is easy to become confused about the aircraft's attitude and direction during the flick roll as the horizon may not be in view. If there is any doubt, centralise the controls and recover from the dive. You may be steeply inverted at the completion of the roll. A pull-through will consume a great amount of altitude and may result in excessive speed. Roll to the nearest horizon and recover. Manage the throttle and RPM.

Derry Turn

Description

The Derry turn was named after the test pilot, John Derry, who used the manoeuvre to demonstrate the DH 110 (the prototype of the Sea Vixen) at Farnborough.

The manoeuvre consists of a steep turn in one direction reversed via a roll under – through the inverted position to a steep turn in the opposite direction.

The roll itself is nominally an aileron roll, but depending on airspeed, large amounts of rudder may be required to counter the adverse yaw, and the manoeuvre can be most unbalanced. It sounds simple and it looks spectacular in a heavy fighter, especially at lower speeds, but it can be fraught with danger near the ground.

Piloting Technique

Start from a normal steep turn with full power. A visual feature may be used for the reversal. When there is about 15° to go, the back pressure is relaxed and the aircraft is rolled under with full aileron and proverse rudder until the opposite 60° bank angle is reached. The roll is stopped and the g is reapplied. Simple.

Points of Airmanship

It is essential to release the back pressure before applying the aileron and rudder or we suddenly have full pro-spin controls. Further, imagine if the airspeed is low. . .

Chapter 7

An Aerobatic Sequence

Developing an aerobatic sequence is not only challenging but makes better use of airborne time, better use of airspace and gives a better opportunity to develop anticipation and orientation. Also, the best way to return to aerobatic flying after a break is to have your own flight sequence of manoeuvres, which you can perform and develop until it becomes polished and professional. You can develop a second, more advanced sequence for later stages when you are in current practice. Further, your own sequence will reflect your own taste, skill and preferences.

Designing the Sequence

Start with a piece of paper and draw a line representing the axis of the sequence which will be the reference line feature on the ground. We will choose a feature into wind or otherwise accept any displacement that occurs during the duration of the sequence. You may use your own symbols or perhaps you would like to adopt the now universal code for aerobatics, called the Aresti system of notation. Choose, say, five core manoeuvres that will be linked.

Let's take an example:
- Take a loop, barrel roll, aileron roll, stall turn, slow roll with a pause at the inverted position, and an avalanche. We can use the stall turn as a linking manoeuvre and even add another one, if desired.
- From the line feature, we will plan to start with potential energy of say 2,000 ft above the minimum altitude and we will run in at 90° to the reference line so that we can have a good look for other aircraft.

The *HASELL* checks will be done well before this.

For our aircraft all manoeuvres are eas-ier to the left and with side-by-side seat-ing, so we will plan to begin with a wing-over to the left to line up with the feature and at the same time set the attitude and power and establish the entry speed for the first manoeuvre. We can see better, for other traffic, too.

The easiest manoeuvre to begin with, and the one with the lowest entry speed, is the aileron roll. From a left wing-over it doesn't matter which way we roll as there will be a pause for a straight pull-up before the roll. We will roll left.

- From the left roll, we will pause and then pull–up into a right-hand wing-over through 225° to offset the line for a pull-up into a left-hand barrel roll.
- From the barrel roll, we will continue directly into a left wing-over to line up on the feature for a loop.
- The exit dive from a loop is a good entry point for a stall turn – which we will do to the left.
- From the stall turn we will pull up smoothly into an avalanche and a further stall turn.
- Exit from the stall turn will be controlled to contain the airspeed and we'll pull up slightly, pause and then roll to inverted, pause for 5 seconds and roll erect. To provide a deliberate ending to the sequence, we will waggle the wings to indicate that we are complete when the aircraft is straight-and-level and all applied g is removed.

What Do You Think?

It's hard work but good fun and great training. The whole sequence would have taken about 5 minutes. Once the sequence is designed, consider if the continuity and flow is OK - and if the direction of the manoeuvres allow for a smooth flow. Modify if necessary and then pace it out on the ground.

Draw Mud-Maps and Do a Rain Dance

Practise the sequence on the ground by walking through the sequence around a line in the dirt - a true 'mud map' of your aerobatic sequence – and saying the manoeuvres attitudes, entry speeds and power settings as you go. It's a wonderful way to ingrain the sequence and the necessary actions. Include where to look in your rehearsal and say the sequence out loud. This is called over-learning and part-task training. It is a known and valuable learning process. (Yes, aerobatic pilots can appear happily insane.)

Aresti Notation

Colonel Jose Aresti was a world-renowned competition aerobatic pilot who approached flying in a scientific manner. He developed a notation for manoeuvres which has become the international standard. It has been expanded to include a scoring system with degree of difficulty applied to each manoeuvre.

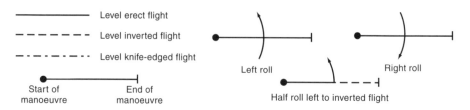

The Aresti notation includes a particular type of line to represent the aircraft's attitude, and then a series of symbols to illustrate the particular manoeuvre as follows.

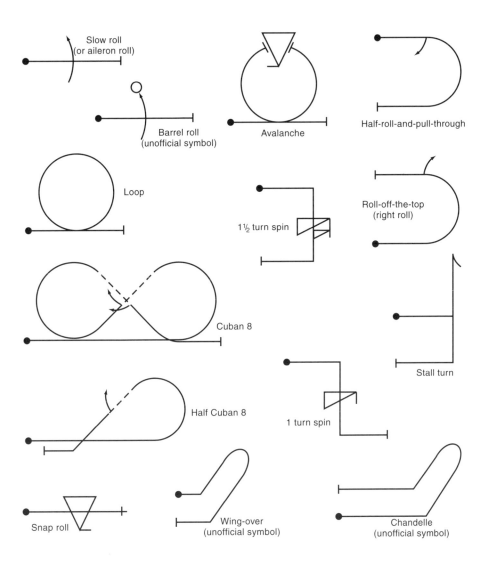

If we wanted to illustrate the sequence we used above, it would look like this:

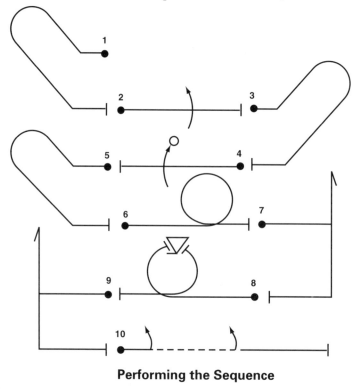

Performing the Sequence

Tips

- Use a ground reference line - into wind.
- A clear horizon all round.
- Use wing-overs early.
- Use the wing-overs to position, to look out, and to establish the line, the attitude and the entry speed for the next manoeuvre.
- Don't fuss too much with altitude as long as you are comfortably above 3,000 feet. (Don't pull hard to be out by say 4,000 if the induced drag will prejudice the entry speed for the next manoeuvre.)
- Use left wing-over into right roll so it flows - and right roll into right wing-over.
- Plan the wing-over for offset line for a barrel roll, e.g. loop into right wing-over into left barrel roll (225° change of direction).
- If things fall apart, return to straight-and-level. Don't fly from one error and allow it to compound into the next.
- Start with excess altitude rather than finish with inadequate energy.
- If you can't make the entry speed by the required altitude, stop and climb and start again. Don't start a manoeuvre with inadequate energy and expect to stagger through it.

Chapter 8

A Basic Aerobatic Training Programme

Introduction

The following programme was developed over a number of years and was popular as it offered a gentle and controlled introduction to aerobatics and allowed the student to develop a tolerance, understanding, feel and expectation for manoeuvring, at the same time as the skills and knowledge of the aircraft were developed. It was developed around the CAP 10, and it may be that for your aircraft type a different sequence of increasingly difficult manoeuvres may be appropriate.

There may also be a need to conduct an initial tailwheel conversion.

Teaching Aerobatics

The student will become confident if you are and if it shows. Don't try to teach unless you yourself are current on the type and the manoeuvres. If you love flying and you love aerobatics, the student will also – it's as simple as that. If you criticise some aircraft types or avoid some manoeuvres, the student will inherit the same bias and caution.

Don't try to impress the student with your ability. Try to teach him or her so well that they impress you with their ability to fly – and therefore they reflect your ability to instruct. Don't scare them and don't let them scare themselves (or you) until they have a degree of proficiency and you are sure they will ultimately cope with the developing situation.

Coax them through the exercises and encourage them. Don't be over-critical until they are consistently safe and you know their ability should produce more accurate or polished results. Always promote early recognition and correction of potential loss-of-control and completion of the manoeuvre rather than a series of unusual attitude recoveries – although they must be fully capable of ultimately recovering from such situations.

Pick a progression of demand and difficulty so that they can show improvement and competence. It is easy to set a task that is beyond them and so reduce their confidence and pleasure. There will be the occasional over-confident student but they will soon realise the reality as you let them progress to more difficult exercises and you criticise fairly their acceptance of any standards that are less than those of which they are capable. If their confidence exceeds their ability, the aircraft, and the manoeuvres, will show it. One way is to progress from a steep turn to a wing-over, to an aileron roll from a wing-over entry, then to a loop, barrel roll and inverted flight. Then join some basic manoeuvres together in a short sequence. Use a line feature into wind.

General Description of the Programme

To develop confidence, piloting skill and a tolerance to manoeuvring, we will approach the training programme in a logical and safe way. We will first refresh your flying at low speed and high angles of attack, high speed and low angles of attack, and for the first time high speed and high angles of attack.

We'll begin with a refresher on steep turns and managing the energy of the aircraft in sustained turning. We'll see what limits there are for our aircraft and we'll explore flying at speeds above and below V_A. We'll progressively build up load factors and manoeuvre rates as we go along. A logical sequence to follow begins with a refresher on steep turns, and we will revisit flying at low speed, high angle of attack, in both straight and level flight and while turning.

We also look at the highest-speed end of the aircraft's flight envelope, and for the first time we'll look at high speed and high angle of attack. We'll conduct a refresher on unusual or extreme attitude recoveries, nose high and nose low, and we'll look at stalling and departure from control flight. The value of doing these exercises is to refresh the feel and characteristics of the particular aircraft at the extremes of this flight envelope.

Then, we'll start the aerobatic course as such. The first and probably the most important manoeuvre is the wing-over. The wing-over is the positioning and linking manoeuvre and is essential for all aerobatic sequences. It's also extremely valuable to introduce the behaviour of the aircraft, as it accelerates, decelerates, nose-high attitude, nose-low attitude, high air speed, low air speed, and it's a wonderful refresher or a way of getting to know an aircraft type that you haven't flown before. From the wing-over, we progress to the simple aileron roll.

Next, the loop, the barrel roll and the stall turn. Then we'll link these manoeuvres together in a sequence, so that we can flow from one to the next.

Once the positive g manoeuvres are mastered, we'll gently explore inverted flight and the first of the negative g manoeuvres, the slow roll.

We'll also look at joined manoeuvres, and if the aircraft has sufficient performance, upward rolls and downward rolls. We'll then link rolling and looping manoeuvres into the Cuban eight and the roll-off-the-top.

Finally we'll put these additional manoeuvres into one sequence. At this level, all of the manoeuvres will be done in the training area above 3,000 feet and we will use a ground reference, purely to orient ourselves. No attempt will be made to position the sequence in relation to a point on the ground; that is to say, we'll ignore the effect of wind for the time being.

Detailed Sequence of Instruction

A suggested programme is detailed as follows:

Flight Zero – Tailwheel Endorsement (If Appropriate)

Description
The introduction to a tailwheel configuration is an important first step for many aerobatic pilots. While the handling of the aircraft is identical, the take-off, landing and the ground handling are significantly different. The tailwheel aircraft requires a greater degree of control and anticipation. This in itself is a valuable first step in becoming a competent aerobatic pilot.

Points of Airmanship
Prevent any yaw early. Fly accurate speeds, especially at the runway threshold. Discuss the appropriate technique for the aircraft (three-point or tail-down wheeler) and crosswind techniques. Include sideslipping approaches if appropriate.

Flight One – Aircraft Type Familiarisation or Refresher
The introduction to your aerobatic aircraft is a vital part of the aerobatic endorsement, and if this is shallow then you will become neither confident nor competent in the more demanding manoeuvres. Take your time in getting to know the aircraft type thoroughly.

The introduction should include:
- familiarisation with speeds, power settings and limitations;
- the flight envelope (V-n diagram);
- V_A;
- weight and balance;
- emergency procedures; and
- restarting the engine in flight.

The flight should include:
- familiarisation with the aerobatic training area and routes;
- practising forced landings;
- maintaining balanced flight with airspeed and power changes and with aileron application at high and low airspeeds;
- high- and low-speed handling;
- manoeuvring on the buffet/manoeuvring at a set value of g;
- manoeuvring at high angles of attack at high and low airspeeds;
- unusual attitude recoveries; and
- stalling and departures.

Description

Introduction to the wing-over and chandelle:

- power settings and trim;
- attitudes;
- using a line reference;
- progressively steeper wing-overs with more rapid control inputs and more extreme attitudes;
- completing the wing-over on line and with the entry attitude for a following manoeuvre; and
- alternate joined wing-overs.

Points of Airmanship

Hand-over/take-over procedures. Lookout. Looking ahead of the manoeuvres. Strapping-in. Sick bag. No loose objects. HASELL checks.

Flight Two – The Aileron Roll and Loop

Description

Having gained a degree of familiarity and confidence in manoeuvring the aircraft and having developed a feel for the stall boundary, the next step is to turn the aircraft upside-down while maintaining positive g.

Depending on the aircraft type it may be easier to begin with the loop, but if possible, the aileron roll is a softer introduction for the student. Use the wing-over as the clearing and set-up manoeuvre and build on the previous sortie.

Stress the importance of setting the trim and feeling the feedback through the controls. The loop needs a firm but not violent application of g, a straight pull-up and then minor adjustment for balance, alignment and buffet. Look back early for the far horizon over the top and be ready to slightly relax the back pressure to avoid excessive buffet. Control the RPM and reinstate the back pressure as the aircraft accelerates.

The aileron roll can be entered as for the wing-over, and when the nose-high attitude is reached, stop the pitching and apply the aileron positively. In most trainers, full aileron will be needed. Simply complete the 360° rotation. Initially keep whatever fore or aft pressure was needed to check the pitching. Later, apply a little forward pressure from the 45° before, to 45° after, the inverted attitude.

Points of Airmanship

The control inputs should now be firm and confident but not violent. Keep the head and eyes looking where the aircraft is going to be going. Stress the need for vertical space and a clear horizon. The lookout needs to cover a larger area of sky, also vertically. Especially point out blind spots for the aircraft type. Revise the physiological aspects of g.

Flight Three – The Barrel Roll and Stall Turn

Description
In many ways, this sortie is the most pleasant and yet the most challenging. Refresh the previous lesson and revisit the manoeuvres.

The stall turn is straightforward, having the same entry and the same recovery as the loop. Try for a truly vertical climb, or a little beyond, apply full rudder and then use aileron to prevent a roll into the direction of yaw. Control the RPM in the dive.

The likelihood with the barrel roll is that the entry attitude will not be high enough and the aircraft will lose a great deal of altitude through the second half of the roll. Also, there is a tendency to relax the aileron application, when it should be slightly increased with reducing airspeed. As a result, the roll-rate will slow over the top. Increased back pressure combined with relaxed aileron is required for the last quarter of the roll. Balance is a finesse that will come with practice.

Points of Airmanship
Vertical recovery technique should be revised. Engine handling should be emphasised for the aircraft type. Actions in the event of the engine stopping should be discussed.

Flight Four – Half Rolls, Inverted Flight and the Complete Slow Roll

Description
Use the previously practised entry to the aileron roll and stop the aircraft at the wings-level inverted position. Illustrate and maintain the inverted level flight attitude with forward stick. Stress the stick position and force required. Complete and aileron roll to erect flight, progressively relaxing the forward pressure to the wings-vertical position and then applying slight back pressure for the last 90° of the roll.

The complete slow roll is best built with a pause at the inverted position to ensure that the second half starts from the correct point. The second half of the roll is the more difficult, and if the correct inverted flight attitude is not achieved, it becomes impossible.

Points of Airmanship
This is the first sortie with negative g and should be approached cautiously to maintain the student's confidence. A clean and tidy cockpit helps considerably. Emphasise strapping-in correctly and firmly. No loose objects.

Flight Five – The Cuban Eight, Roll-off-the-Top and Avalanche

Description

The Cuban eight is a pleasant combination of the loop and aileron roll. The roll-off-the-top requires a higher g, positive pull-up and a higher entry speed. The roll should be commenced as the aircraft reaches the inverted flight attitude, when full aileron and balancing rudder is applied. Adverse aileron yaw can be pronounced. The back pressure is removed immediately before the aileron is applied but don't try to apply the firm forward pressure required for inverted flight.

The avalanche is an exciting and easy manoeuvre to perform. Emphasise the benefit of accelerating the aircraft into the buffet and stall well before the inverted flight attitude.

Points of Airmanship

Two areas which offer a risk of departure are the roll-off-the-top when full aileron and significant rudder is applied at very low airspeed. It is important that the back pressure is removed so that the angle of attack is not close to the stalling angle when the roll is commenced. The flick roll at the top of the avalanche is safe if it is commenced early and the aircraft is pulled positively into the buffet. It should not be commenced once the inverted attitude is past, as the airspeed will build quickly and the aircraft limits may be exceeded. There is a risk of disorientation during the roll and it is initially difficult to recover to the line feature.

Flight Six – A Basic Aerobatic Sequence

Description

For me the greatest pleasure in flying comes from a practised and controlled aerobatic sequence. It's not unlike a choreographed aerial ballet. Use a line feature and stress the anticipation needed to be planning the entry for the next manoeuvre while still conducting its precedent.

Points of Airmanship

Emphasise firm but gentle control. Look out. Think ahead of the aircraft – feel the cues. Use a line feature and a clear horizon. Discuss escape routes from any and every stage of the sequence.

Afterword

Advanced Manoeuvring

The intention of this book was to interest and possibly excite you enough to enter the world of aerobatic flight. If you have, I need say no more. You may be happy to stay at this stage of flying aerobatics for pleasure, as I am, or you may wish to proceed further to competition and advanced manoeuvres. If you do, I would recommend Neil Williams's excellent book, *Aerobatics*, published by Airlife.

• Now that you have become competent at basic aerobatic manoeuvres, I would also like to add a word of caution – the next step is a *doosie*.

• You must not, can not, should not, please don't, attempt advanced or ground-referenced manoeuvres without experience and without specialised instruction. These manoeuvres are beyond the skill-level of most pilots – including airline pilots and military pilots without special training. This is the realm of the specialist competition and display pilot, and it's a profession of its own.

Manoeuvring Relative to the Ground – The Effects of Wind

When aerobatics are performed for a judge or for a crowd, then they have to be oriented to a reference line on the ground and one that is unlikely to be into wind. Thus, all manoeuvres have to be modified by continuously changing conditions. A loop becomes an offset loop – one wing up, one wing down. The aircraft has to track down a reference line which is not aligned with the roll-axis of the aircraft. You are not allowed to fly over the crowd, yet, sure-as-eggs, the wind will blow you towards the crowd during your low-level turns, so that you are flying to the limit to stay clear – and the induced drag is spoiling your excess energy. Add to this, excitement, stress, nerves – and stir gently. You can see that this is a special arena.

Back to Earth

Enough of this fantasising – let's go back to our basic aerobatic manoeuvres at a safe altitude. Everyone who has ever been a good and complete pilot started here. Learn them well. Take care of yourself and your aircraft.

I know you'll enjoy it as much as I.

Index